A Fast Bike to Byzantium

Andy C Wareing

Copyright

Contents

In memory of my dear old Mum and Dad, who never stopped me from doing one single thing that I thought I could do, even when they should have really just said no.

A Border Incident

The young border guard had a scar shaped like a question mark below the squint of his left eye.

He had cropped hair, dark beneath his peaked cap, soft stubble in patches across his young cheeks. He held a matte black Kucher K-1 submachine gun nestled securely under the damp sweat stained arc of his armpit. The scored and worn brown leather sling was taut around the faded olive-green collar of his tunic.

I was far from being any sort of expert in early 1980's Hungarian armaments, but my new friend had the barrel so close under my chin that I could easily read the name of the weapon stamped crudely onto the oiled steel. I could also smell the cordite that seeped like a threat from the rifled muzzle of the weapon.

He held out a hand. "Vízum és útlevél." He demanded in a harsh language I did not understand.

He had narrow pale lips, as strict as scripture. His ebony eyes were without expression.

It seemed logical to me that he was asking for paperwork. I was still sat astride the big Suzuki, engine thrumming and popping in the morning heat of the day. To the right of me a long snaking line of saloon cars, mostly Audis and Mercedes, were making their way in single file towards the two fortified gates that would take us out of the demilitarized zone from Austria, and into the communist held Eastern bloc of Hungary; out of free Europe to slip behind the Iron Curtain of the USSR.

The gates were topped by razor wire, set amid two lofty guard towers, where indistinct silhouettes paced, staring out into the sun, searching for targets. In each tower a heavy machine gun had its barrel pointing lazily to the sky.

"Vizum!" He demanded once more.

I turned the ignition off with a sigh. I carefully, and slowly, reached into the black leather tank bag in front of me, to retrieve my passport which held all the visa stamps that I had diligently collected over the preceding three months in anticipation of this trip.

I held out the royal blue British passport with supreme confidence, a citizen of the commonwealth. After all, on the inside of the passport was elegantly and commandingly written, '*Her Britannic Majesty's Secretary of State requests and requires in the name of Her Majesty all those whom it may concern allow the bearer to pass freely without let or hindrance.*'

The very voice of Queen Elizabeth II, reached in plummy tones across the miles that separated her wayward citizen from her queenly and protective bosom.

My heavily armed and frowning Hungarian friend seemed not to have been made aware of Her Majesty's personal assurance of my safe passage as he rifled through the pages one by one, only to hand it back to me with a shake of his head.

He narrowed his eyes even more, fingered the trigger guard of his submachine gun as he did so. He took a step back to eye me with renewed interest. The day was warm, the sun already high in the cerulean sky, and yet I had to acknowledge that I was incongruously dressed in very wet clothes. Steam rose from me, like the touch of the sun on the last racehorse home. He glanced down at the hole in the knee of my jeans and the broad, dark ring of drying blood that surrounded it.

I could see him slowly try to process my condition and dishevelled state of dress. If it were possible, his eyes narrowed even more. At this rate it wouldn't be long before he couldn't see me at all. I could almost hear his thought process as the slow cogs turned.

Who was this curiously damp and bloody interloper from the west?

"Vizum? Visa?" He stated bluntly.

I knew the visa was stamped and stapled inside the passport. I had personally obtained it from the Hungarian consulate two months ago.

Part of the problem was that I had chosen to transit Hungary in a not particularly convivial era.

The year was 1986. Eastern Europe was still held firmly in the iron grasp of the USSR. Closed borders and communism pervaded. All things western were viewed through the lens of fear and suspicion. But I had been more than diligent in my preparation, aware that a mistake with the paperwork would result in being turned back at one of the normally closed borders.

"Visa. Yes," I said, "here."

I thumbed through the pages myself until I located the official looking, colourfully resplendent stamped insert. It was clearly labelled 'Vizum' with the word 'Magyarország' beneath.

"Visa. Hungary. See for yourself, it is right here!"

I offered it back to him; certain he had missed it in his initial search. I pointed at the visa. I didn't know any

Hungarian, but I had a little French and even un poco de Español, which at that point I deemed to be better than nothing.

"Voici mon visa," I said pointing, "Ici. Aqui."

The guard's face was a blank wall, implacable.

"Nem vizum," he said motioning me to dismount from the bike with the menacing barrel of his weapon.

With a muffled sigh of frustration and the beginning of some real concern, I pushed the kickstand down with my left leg and swung my right leg over the seat, carefully lowering the bike to rest as I did so. The young guard annoyingly tapped me on the helmet with the knuckles of his right hand and gestured for me to remove it. My hands shook a little as I undid the chin strap and pulled the lid from my head. It was already hot, and the sweat dripped into my eyes. I placed the helmet on the tank bag.

"Gyere velem. Come. Viz me," he said.

Time slowed. I saw his finger slip inside the trigger guard. His fingernails were bitten, knuckles white with tension. His index finger not quite touching the trigger, not yet ready to shoot, but happy to do so if this ignorant tourist put up any type of a struggle. Perhaps happy even for the chance to do so, anything to relieve the boredom of his relentless guard duty.

I could feel the hot sun burning through my thinning hair, see the eyes of the Austrian drivers queueing to cross into Hungary, to visit their friends and family who had been caught on the wrong square miles of land when their country had been annexed at the end of World War II. Their eyes watched me wide and staring as the gun barrel was pushed into a kidney, forced me to walk away from my bike and all of my belongings. A comedic, tragic distraction to *their* safe journey, something remote, happening to a stranger. They still safe in their own steel cages, secretly delighted perhaps that this was not happening to them or their families. Not their concern.

The boy with the question mark scar, I was beginning to just think of him as Mark at this point, gestured with the barrel of his gun and we began to walk across to a low concrete building with a green painted corrugated steel roof and, as my heart rate began to race, I realized the extent of my predicament.

I was a child of the 1960's. Born in 1965 to be precise. The year Lyndon B Johnson became president, Winston Churchill died, and Muhammad Ali knocked out Sonny Liston. For the first time in my safe western life, I felt the sudden personal isolation inherent of my generation. The era when personal cell phones were a piece of science fiction that lay in the distant realm of phasers, tricorders, and transporters; a Sci-Fi dream set twenty years in the future. No pagers, no email, no text, no phones. No tracking, no Global Positioning System, no Google maps, no find my iPhone. No find Andy.

Not a single soul on the planet knew where I was, where I had come from, or where I had been heading.

I held on tightly to my passport, but my keys were still in the ignition of my motorcycle, the rest of my paperwork, traveller's cheques and cash held in a jumbled combination of German Marks, French Francs, Yugoslavian Dinar, Turkish Lira and Greek Drachma stored in my unsecured tank bag.

Question Mark nudged me forward with the barrel of the Kucher K-1 and the blood in my veins ran cold.

To say this day was not going well, may have, at that point, been something of an understatement.

A Rough Beginning

In fact, so far, this year's entire trip had not been going well.

In my late teens and early twenties, before I knew any better and lacked the funds for any more comfortable alternative, every year I would put myself through a personal hell by picking a remote and challenging destination to which I would ride a motorcycle to.

I would fastidiously pool all of my available holiday leave and typically, in a three-week window or less, I would pack a tent, a sleeping bag, a little Calor gas burner, billy can and several chicken and mushroom pot noodles, and set off on my own. It wasn't that I loved to ride solo, although to be fair it had its advantages. I was usually alone because the places I picked were far and difficult to get to, and back from, in such a short space of time.

When I asked my fellow biker friends if they would like to accompany me on my travels, the usual response was a loud snort and a firm, "fuck no, we're all going to Ayia Napa to get pissed and shag birds."

Which to be honest was a very fair and balanced response.

The year of this story, 1986, I had chosen Istanbul in distant Turkey. If you assume I had selected it because of its rich culture and history, or its fine cuisine and architecture, or that through its long history the city had once been a beacon of the Silk Road and had held several different names, firstly Byzantium, then Constantinople and now, in the modern era, Istanbul, you would be mistaken.

I knew nothing about the city other than part of it lay inside Europe and part in Asia. That single fact intrigued me to such an extent that I had to go and see it for myself. To ride across the Bosporus suspension bridge. To cross a continent.

The trip had begun, as things often do, in an ordinarily satisfactory enough manner. I had packed the bike in the front yard of my Mum and Dad's house and then without a backward glance I had set off, map folded under the transparent cover of my tank bag, passports, money, and ferry tickets carefully stowed.

An easy ride across the cloud soaked and sheep speckled hills of the Pennines, from Southport to Hull, mostly on the M62. I watched the sun begin to darken the sky in front of me as it simultaneously painted the canvas of the western sky aflame in my rear-view mirrors.

Rain burdened clouds rolled close to shore, keen to release their contents onto the perpetually rain slicked city streets as I arrived at my destination. Full night, like a heavy blanket had fallen as I navigated the approach roads to King George dock on the north side of the Humber. The North Sea ferry MV Norstar lay bathed by spotlights, in berth waiting for its passengers, mostly HGV's and the occasional car. Mine was the only motorcycle, and the boarding crew waved me to the front of the queue to wait for the loading doors to lower.

MV Norstar was a 'roll-on/roll-off' type ferry. 27,000 tons, purposefully built to be as wide as she could possibly be, while allowing an inch or two on either side to allow her to navigate the locks just outside her berth. The design of the ferry used large watertight doors at both the rear and the front of the ship to be opened to admit and exit vehicles in an efficient and speedy manner. The design was always known to be high-risk, as the construction at the time incorporated not a single watertight compartment to limit flooding. Even in the industry they were jokingly referred to as 'roll-on/roll-off/roll-over' ferries.

Indeed in March 1987, less than one year after the boat I was waiting to board set sail, the MS Herald of Free Enterprise left the Belgium port of Zeebrugge on her scheduled night-time sailing to Dover only to, almost immediately, capsize. Incredibly, the boarding doors had been accidently left wide open. The cause was primarily the poor design of the ship. But the accident still wouldn't have happened if it hadn't been initiated by the behaviour of those pesky and inevitably flawed human creatures.

It was the duty of the boatswain to ensure the doors were safely and securely closed but, on this evening, the assistant boatswain, Mark Stanley, felt fatigued after cleaning the car deck on his own and had left his post for, what he considered to be, a well-earned nap. He was still fast asleep in his cabin when the harbour-station call was sounded, and the moorings were dropped.

The first officer, Leslie Sabel was on deck and tasked with staying in place until he could visually see that the doors were closed. Unfortunately, Sabel was under enormous pressure to resume his duties on the bridge. He left when he saw Mark Stanley approaching. Unfortunately, he was mistaken. Stanley was still asleep in his cabin.

Another member of the crew, Terence Ayling, was the last person on the deck and saw with his own eyes that the doors lay open to the sea as the ship departed its moorings. He was the last of the crew who could have saved the ship from its imminent doom. When asked at the subsequent inquest why he didn't close the doors or raise the alarm, he responded simply, that that wasn't his job.

The Herald of Free Enterprise left her berth in Zeebrugge's inner harbour just after six in the evening. She carried a crew of 80 and was transporting 459 passengers, 81 cars, 3 buses and 47 trucks. As she left the comparative safety of the inner harbour, she had only four minutes left. From the moment water began to flood the ship, she took only 90 seconds to capsize, drowning 193 people, most of whom were trapped inside, in darkness and confusion, as the freezing water rose to overcome them.

With that cheery thought, all still thankfully three years in the future, I watched the doors creak and clank open and rode up the slippery ramp to find a bulkhead to which I could strap the bike against. As we had waited, a squall had risen from the North Sea and the ship could already be felt to heave and rock against her moorings. I cinched up the loading straps as tight as I could and grabbed my tank bag and leather panniers and climbed the steep steel stairs out of the vehicle hold and into the passenger compartment.

The ship did provide basic, windowless, private cabins strategically situated only feet above the engine rooms. But even these were far beyond my limited means. For the eleven-hour sailing across the North Sea to Rotterdam I had reserved a reclining chair at the front of the ship and close to the dining room. I stowed the belongings I wouldn't need in a locker, found my allotted chair, and flung my leather jacket and helmet across it to make sure it screamed 'THIS IS MINE – BUGGER OFF,' and headed to the dining room.

The dining room was a vast space the entire width of the ship. In the centre was a double-sided food console with steaming hot trays, each filled to brimming; one with potatoes, one with vegetables, others with thick carved slices of chicken, beef, and pork. There were pasta and chips, sausages, meat pies spilling juices, Yorkshire puddings, and at the end, a huge lake of bubbling gravy. I grabbed the biggest plate I could find and started to pile up the food. As I balanced the food increasingly precariously on my plate, the engines of the ship rose in pitch and the infrastructure around me hummed and vibrated as the ship pulled against its moorings.

The dining room was quiet, perhaps only a third full, with a few other diners slowly trickling in. I grabbed a seat by the window on the port side of the ship, so that I could watch the shore slip away as we headed down the Humber and out towards open water. As soon as we were free of the dock the ship began to roll gently, and forty minutes later, as I wiped the gravy from my chin, I looked out of the window to see Spurn Point and the bright orange Humber RLNI Lifeboat Station slip by to be replaced by white topped breakers and a sea that was darkly indiscernible from the tumultuous sky above.

As soon as I stood from my little table and looked around me, I quickly realized two things. This ferry was really starting to rise and roll in an increasingly disorienting manner as it crested each heavy wave and crashed into its partnering trough, and the dining room was entirely empty. I staggered across the rolling floor and found a door that led outside and out into the open air. The door was heavy but as I released the catch the wind snatched it from me and blew it with a loud clang against the external bulkhead.

Outside, free of the natural breakwater of Spurn Point, only the open sea lay on either side. I staggered on the slippery, salt rimed deck and desperately grabbed onto the cold steel rail with white-knuckled hands. Wild stallions thrashed the ocean into angry white peaks. Columns of water towered over us and crashed against the ship. In one second the ocean roiled only feet from my nose, and in the next, the sky swung lazily to replace it. Ice cold salt spray lashed my face and drenched me. Again, and again the ship rolled hard on its side just as its prow dug deep into the crashing wave ahead and pulled the ship dizzyingly forward, hard against its own inertia. Then the ocean released the bow and we swung hard to starboard as the prow rose in its desperate attempt to crest the next wave.

It seemed prudent to wrestle the door shut before I was swept into the salty melee to never be seen again. Back inside, I had to hold onto tables that were bolted to the floor, to stagger, knees bent to roll myself gingerly out of the dining room.

Back in the passenger quarters I stumbled into a scene from Dante's nine circles of hell. That is if the first five circles were vomit, despair, spew, hurl, and tears.

I had arrived just in time to witness the beginning of a bilious chain reaction. One woman with both of her hands filled by those of her toddler daughters had stalled in her attempt to reach the bathrooms. She had realized, too late, that it was a toilet bowl far too far and had frozen, stock still in the middle of the crowded space. Her brow was ashen and flecked with beads of sweat, her cheeks turned a pale shade of green and then billowed out like those of a bull frog about to issue a spectacularly loud mating call. Once filled, her cheeks had only one recourse left. She hurled the contents of her stomach, like some sickly fire hydrant to spatter loudly across her shoes, the shoes of her sweet, innocent infant daughters, and much of the slick tiled floor. Already nauseous, with barely a breath between them, her daughters followed suit and added their lunches to the melee.

Shouts and shrieks of dismay rang around the room as people rushed to move away from the liquid piles now compelled into almost lifelike and sinister motion by the rolling of the ship. Like spilt vegetable soup, the steaming puddles began to pursue people around the room, pinning some into corners and quickly out running the weakest of the herd. Parents dragged their own screaming children, pushed others rudely out of the way.

People already rendered queasy began to retch, burp and hurp. A vast exodus to the bathrooms was already underway, but their capacity was swiftly outstripped, the floor became the only refuge for stomachs jollied into motion by the ships continued instability and the increasing miasma.

Chunks and bile flowed freely. Grown men were dropped to their knees as stomachs cramped. The sound of chundering and subsequent spattering echoed around the once sterile space.

I admit the sour stench and sight of so much vomit made me feel a tad liverish myself. I manfully swallowed a gloop of rising bile that tasted strangely of gravy and roast beef, tiptoed carefully through the streaming, steaming pools to grab my leather jacket and helmet and made my escape back into the empty dining room.

I wedged my jacket between my head and the humming, madly vibrating window, and fell into a fitful sleep, one filled with animated and murderous piles of spew, with carrots for eyes, that pursued me down malodorous panic filled corridors.

Cat Nap

The clanging of food trays and the smell of cooked bacon finally woke me. I wouldn't say that I had the best night's sleep. The doors to the dining room were intermittently caught by the wind when one of the crew opened an external door. The sound boomed and reverberated down the long and empty room, intermittently rousing me from an uneasy slumber.

I needed a pee, so with a stretch and a crack of a neck stiffened by my awkward sleeping position I made my way out of the dining room. The passenger compartment was quiet and subdued compared to the pungent fracas of the previous evening. The cleaning crew had completed a mammoth task and every surface gleamed. The acrid tang of bleach was an assuring assault on the nostrils. Bodies lay sprawled in chairs and on the floor, faces pale with exhaustion, tinted lime by latent nausea and personal tribulation. Low moans and groans of discomfort and anguish were the only sounds, the soundtrack to a low budget zombie movie.

Back in the dining room I was one of only three or four people sufficiently awake and with a stomach calm and steady enough to brave the breakfast. Outside the storm had passed us by, or perhaps the ships steady progress had finally outrun it, left it in our turbulent wake to trouble the trawlermen as we slipped, now smoothly, from Dogger and into German Bight.

The morning sea was a flat calm, and the watery sun was doing it best to break free of a line of pink marshmallow topped clouds that sat close to the horizon. I got a warm plate and piled up some bacon, sausage, mushrooms, and scrambled eggs. There must have been three or four hundred people onboard, and the price for breakfast was built into the fare, but I suspected it would be the seagulls who would be fat and happy this morning, flapping hard to keep up with the ship and its nutritious wake.

With breakfast done I took a walk outside. The day was cool, and I shrugged into my leather jacket and zipped it tight against a light but chilly wind. The breeze from the south brought the scent of the commercial districts of The Hague and Rotterdam along with the harsh calls of seabirds across the sea. In the distance, the smoky oil refinery and hoisting crane speckled outline of the Port of Rotterdam rose above the flat landscape, a dark smudge just visible on the horizon.

I had a good long ride to complete so went back inside the dining room and packed a banana, three bread rolls and a big pile of salami and cheese inside some napkins and wedged them into my helmet. Nobody else was eating it and I had, after all, already paid for it. Pay for a breakfast—get a free lunch, as good a motto to live by as any other, that's what I say.

I grabbed my tank bag and paniers from the lockbox just as the shipboard klaxon announced that all drivers needed to return to their vehicles. I hauled all of my gear down the steep steel stairs, back into the hold of the ship. I made sure the magnets gripped the tank bag tightly to the tank while I gave the bike a quick visual. At least I didn't need to worry about the chain, the big Suzuki transferred power to the back wheel via shaft drive. Wonderful for long distance touring.

I made sure my panniers and tent were secured to the rack at the back of the bike and shook the breadcrumbs from my helmet. I straddled the bike, slipped my lunch into the tank bag, and made sure that my printed map of the Netherlands and Northern Germany was visible and oriented so that I could read it easily through the transparent plastic top of the bag.

I had the route roughly planned in my mind. I had gone over it a thousand times, the same map spread out across my Mums kitchen table, saltshakers and pepper pots pushed to one side. Each red road I had traced with a bitten fingernail. Traced each town, memorized the names and the road numbers that would lead me south and east, down through the breadth of Europe. I had no stops planned. I wanted to wing the whole journey. Ride hard and fast and then either find a campsite or just wild camp by the side of the road. Istanbul was the singular destination to head towards. But outside of that, not a single plan in my mostly empty mind.

My route for the day would take me initially east towards Arnhem before I headed south towards Cologne and Frankfurt. I had been the first to board and given the design of the ship had doors at both the prow and the stern, I would be the first to disembark.

The massive steel doors were slowly lowered. A chink of watery sunshine rushed through the widening gap at the top to instantly transform the bleak, iron, and rust covered interior into a sun dappled cavern filled with dancing motes of dust.

A thousand startled butterflies filled my stomach. The familiar feel of the excitement and anticipation of the first day on the road. I never counted the ride through England to the ferry terminal, so this would be day one of my ride to Istanbul and the very beginnings of Asia.

A boarding steward pointed to me and waved me forward. I nodded back and pulled in the clutch, flipped up the side stand with a practiced kick, fired the engine into life, cogged the bike, into first gear and with a blip of the throttle I was off.

With my heart pounding, and my suddenly dry tongue searching for saliva, I rode carefully down the sea slicked steel ramp all the while muttering to myself, "ride on the right, on the right, on the right."

The ride through the Netherlands was an easy mix of picturesque and tedium. The roads were flat and well paved, the miles ticked by almost unnoticed. Fields glowed with the fragrance and the rainbow brilliance of a million tulips. I passed over broad canals and bridges, flew past windmills and small tidy farmsteads.

Traffic was light and the signs for nearby towns were typically Dutch—Zoetermeer, Hoograven, Driebergen-Rijsenburg, Velhuizen, I played with the unfamiliar mix of vowels and consonant sounds in my head.

I took a short diversion close to Arnhem to cross the John Frost Bridge over the river Nederrijn. This was the famed 'bridge too far' from the World War II movie. A total of 1,750 Allied soldiers died in Operation Market Garden, Montgomery's bold plan to end the war by taking all of the bridges across the major Dutch rivers. If that goal could be achieved, the Siegfried defensive line could be breached and the heart of the German war machine—the Ruhr region could be destroyed. Sadly, Operation Market Garden proved to be literally 'a bridge too far' and ultimately the John Frost Bridge could not be taken, and the assault failed.

Back on the Autobahn I suddenly saw stop lights in the distance and a warning sign that I was approaching the border for Deutschland—Germany.

There are no road borders in Europe anymore. Today, nothing marks the travellers transition from Holland into Germany other than the language change on the road signs. Back in that year, 1986, every country, European or not, had a hard border. One with armed guards, barriers, questions to be asked and answered, paperwork and passports to be diligently checked and marked with an old fashioned but quietly exciting official stamp dipped in black, blue or scarlet ink.

Along with the language change also came a change in currency. In Holland it was the Dutch Guilder. As I crossed the border it became the German Mark. There was something thrilling and romantic about travel in that era. A time before the common usage of credit and debit cards, where cash was king. Of course, the need to carry the currencies of multiple countries was also frustrating and a budgeting headache. ATM machines were only beginning to emerge and only worked in your country of origin, so if you ran short of cash on the road the travellers only option was to find a physical Bureau de Change in a city centre and exchange one currency, or a traveller's cheque, for another currency. It was massively time consuming and costly.

Oh, and you needed to carry a calculator. A real calculator. Remember, no smartphones back then and the exchange rate varied country by country. It varied A LOT. For example, in 1986 you got 3.7 German Marks for each of your lovely British Pounds. In the same year, but in Italy, you would receive 2,700 Italian Lira for every pound coin that sported the stately visage of Her Majesty. A meagre £370 back in 1986 would technically make you a millionaire in Milan, by number if not by fortune.

On this trip alone I would traverse eight different countries. Back home, at my Mum's kitchen table I had carefully calculated where in each country I would need cash for fuel, tolls, camping and supplies. Where possible I would cross an entire country without stopping, to minimize the currencies I would need. Crazy times looking back, but I guess the challenge added a frisson of excitement to every encounter, and it did make life interesting.

Back on the Autobahn my stomach was rumbling so I found a convenient Raststätten or rest stop. Being in Germany, these are regularly provisioned every thirty to sixty kilometres or so apart and, unlike the rest places in America, all have good parking, clean restrooms, petrol stations and at least one restaurant. I had my bread, cheese and salami stored away, so just bought some water, and found a bench seating area in the shade, next to my bike, in which to eat my lunch. As I started to tuck into my feast, my heart sank to see four or five Dutch bikers arrive. They saw the Suzuki and rode across to park up next to me.

I had nothing against other bikers in general or Dutch bikers specifically but as usual they put me to shame in the quality of their kit and attire. All were dressed in the best matching Dainese one-piece leathers and top-notch, super expensive helmets with two-way walkie talkie connections for their beautiful pillion riders. Their bikes, all shining, brand new Ducati's and BMWs. All were equipped with handsome factory-fitted hard panniers and top boxes. The bikers themselves were all blond and tall with hearty tans.

They sat down next to me, instantly making a short, scruffy, balding English biker look immeasurably more like a harangued hobbit than usual. We exchanged greetings and destinations. They were heading east to the Sachsenring motor circuit, not far from the border with Czechoslovakia. They all nodded with something akin to the sympathy one reserves for a simpleton when I told them of my goal.

I looked across at my old and trusty Suzuki GS1000G. I had found an oil leak from the cylinder head only days before I had set off and hadn't had the time to strip the bike and fix it. Oil had seeped out and burnt and blackened the cooling fins of the engine. The aftermarket exhaust was both too loud and too short, it lay like a rusted broken finger beneath the bike. I looked down at my cheap jeans and work boots. My leather jacket with the scuff marks on the shoulders was slung over my helmet, scratched, and already covered in the red streaks of a thousand suicidal bugs. My tent was wrapped in a tattered yellow plastic sack that bore a British Telecom logo, procured from my employer at zero cost. It was tied haphazardly onto the rear rack with three fraying and mismatched bungee cords. It was clear that they thought I might have trouble navigating my way out of the parking lot, never mind all the way to Turkey.

It was always the same on the continent, at least in Holland and Germany. All the riders there had top class kit and were superbly organized. By contrast, you could spot a fellow Brit on the road a mile and a half away. He would be wearing wildly inappropriate gear, mostly held together by Gaffer tape, sat by a motorcycle that looked like it might have been hot-wired and taken from a salvage yard under the cover of darkness, ravenously eating food stolen from a cheap canteen like some feral racoon caught with its head in a bin, and shaking crumbs from his helmet with a puzzled, slightly crazed look on his pale, pimply face.

Back then, in the 1980s, Britain was the pauper of much of Europe. We had already suffered through six years of Thatcherism, endless months of industrial action, the privatization of our utilities, mass unemployment, inflation so high it made Snoop Dog look like the country vicar, and a short but costly distant war with Argentina. At that time France, Germany and even Italy were enjoying far greater GDP growth than Britain.

The Dutch boys asked me if I wanted to ride with them for a few miles, but I was already intimidated and shamed by the experience of their simple proximity, so I bade my grateful farewells and hit the road.

I rode through the afternoon, through the busy industrial heartlands of Dusseldorf, Cologne, and Bonn. As I entered Bavaria, the horizon filled with low rising hills, revealed scatterings of neat villages with ancient baroque buildings, gingerbread pretty against the backdrop of rolling emerald pastures dotted with leaning Bauernhaus chalets and lazy brooks that broke and splashed over granite cobbles. Mile after lazy mile slipped by.

The traffic eased as I passed Frankfurt and the fir trees that grew tall by the sides of the road stole the scenery away, threw a verdant shroud, a magician's cape across the vista.

The day was very warm, the air still, the sun starting to set above the treeline to the west. The smooth road ran straight and without distraction for miles in front of me. The traffic fell away, left me alone, a solitary traveller, the constant rumble of the big four-cylinder bike beneath me a steady reassurance.

For some strange reason I was thinking about Driebergen-Rijsenburg, the town in Holland I had passed earlier in the day. I muttered the name to myself to pass the time, "Driebergen-Rijsenburg."

I repeated it again and again to myself. Muttered the words like a mantra. "Driebergen-Rijsenburg." "Driebergen-Rijsenburg."

It felt comfortable, soothing in its almost hypnotic repetition and unfamiliar tongue-twisting combination of vowels and consonants. Something foreign but reassuring in its cadence...

Suddenly the handlebars vibrated wildly in my hands and the sound of a jack hammer snapped me out of my pleasant reverie.

I had fallen asleep.

The chin piece of my helmet was already rested on the top of my tank bag like some big fat black pillow. My body was slumped forward hands loose on the handlebars. The bike had coasted slowly across into the fast lane and the front tire had hit the rumble strips that marked and separated the edge of the tarmac from the very beginning of eternity.

I woke with a start and an embarrassingly loud and sustained shriek, the sort of noise a six-year-old girl might make when suddenly surprised by a Tarantula leaping from a toy box. I fortunately had the fortitude of mind to not over correct the wobble. Wide-eyed, I eased the throttle and checked my mirrors to navigate safely back across to the inside lane. Luckily the Autobahn was mostly empty. My heart pounded in my chest, and I felt sick to my stomach. I had never once come even close to falling asleep on a motorcycle before. Normally the buffeting weather and vagaries and behaviour of other road users keeps all riders in a state of mind similar to a paranoid, psychopathic frenzy. Without a moment's hesitation I took the very next exit towards the town of Erlangen just north of Nuremberg.

As I had pulled off the main carriageway the sun had dipped and as nightfall crept like a spectre across the horizon, a thin grey gruel of clouds had blown in. A sprinkle of cold rain began to drive droplets to race in a fast arc across the visor of my helmet. The slip road curved around to the right and the new surface water gave the road a brightly reflective sheen, reflected the orange glow of the sodium streetlights. At the intersection a sign pointed left for the town of Obermichelbach and right for Erlangen. Below the sign for Erlangen was a sign shaped like an arrow that pointed towards *Campingplatz Zur Mühle* and I immediately hit my right turn signal.

I was still yawning widely behind the visor that was getting wetter as the rain front swept in from the east, fat droplets accumulated, and the visor began to fog as the temperature dropped.

The number of buildings around me increased, the environment changed from rural to urban and the roads slowly narrowed as I approached the outskirts of Erlangen. To my left I could occasionally glimpse, between the crowded buildings, a steep drop down into the valley of the river Bibert that snaked darkly through the trees. The sun was setting quickly, and the blanket of clouds leached the light from the sky. I scoured ahead, through the fogged visor and the sweeping rain for another sign for the camp site. I had to crack the visor to clear the interior and wiped a gloved hand to smear the rain away.

Up ahead I finally caught sight of another sign for the campground. It directed me take a left turn into a street to my left. I thumbed my indicators and turned left off the main road.

Suddenly I found myself on a narrow-cobbled street that dropped precipitously down to the river. My fatigue disappeared like Casper at an exorcism. The cobbles were bumpy and slick with running rainwater. I dabbed at the front brakes, and they immediately locked the front wheel. I let go and the bike accelerated, pulled down into the gravity well that, if I didn't slow the bike, would end up with me in the river that lay at the very bottom of this long and slippery precipice.

I needed engine braking so cogged it down a gear and the back wheel instantly locked. I pulled in the clutch in a panic to get the bike stabilized and tried again, but no matter how much I slipped the clutch, the rear wheel immediately locked and began to slide across the undulating cobbles. It was like riding across a vast pool of oiled ball bearings.

I had no grip whatsoever. My eyelids were now pulled back so far in fear and concentration that the back of my optic nerve was exposed to, and chilled by, the cold night air. I managed to get the bike into second gear and finally slowed it, stopped it accelerating. I still needed brakes to stop, but every time I touched the front brake the tire locked, and the bike squirmed and slid disconcertingly under me.

A stop sign appeared, twenty yards in front of me, it snared like a barbed fishhook for my attention. A line of trucks was crossing on the street that intersected mine. I panic dabbed the brakes and the bike slid sideways forcing me to counter steer like I was on a dirt bike, not some huge overloaded 1000cc sports bike.

"Fuuuuucckkk," I muttered to myself as the bike slid right and then left. I looked up to see some old chap with a battered homburg and a walrus moustache. He was out walking his Dachshund on a long extending lead in the evening rain. He was stood beneath the stop sign at the intersection trying to cross the road. When he saw me, he reeled his little dog protectively out of the way like he was catching a wild marlin off the coast of Trinidad and Tobago. He stood transfixed watching me. I muttered a whispered "*sorry*" as I slid wide-eyed and sidewards across the junction in front of him.

To my huge relief I slid through a quiet pocket of traffic and the other side of the junction was thankfully paved in tarmac. The bike immediately righted itself and responded to the brakes and I was able to pull over to the side of the road, panting, letting the excess adrenalin drip from every orifice I possessed, and one or two I hitherto had not known existed.

At the very bottom of the hill, I saw another sign for the campsite. I turned left to ride along the bank of the dark river that ran invisible beside me.

The campsite was small and low key. Night had fully eclipsed the landscape, but the rain had thankfully stopped. I put up the tent by torchlight and walked to the little shop on site and bought some unidentifiable tinned meat which I hoped was some type of ham, and a loaf of disconcertingly heavy bread. It had the heft, colour, and texture of a barbeque briquette.

The Germans think bread should use the types of ingredients and be baked in such a way, that it can also be used for general construction material, and this was no different, but I had the foresight to also procure four amber coloured bottles of German pilsner to wash it all down with.

I sat in my little tent, listening to the sounds of the river. With my trusty pocketknife I sawed off chunks of bread and dipped them in what turned out to be a tin of anchovies. As I drained my last pilsner, my exhaustion returned. I zipped up the tent and clambered into my sleeping bag. I placed my jacket over the panniers to create a pillow of sorts and muttering once more the words, "Driebergen-Rijsenburg," I fell into a restive slumber.

A Föhn

Morning brought a bright and clear day. I sat outside my little tent and boiled a cup of water to make instant coffee while I poured over my maps. I needed to be more careful today. For one thing I really didn't need to fall asleep on a speeding motorcycle again. I also had to take sufficient care with the route as I needed to end the day close to Austria's eastern border, to be within close striking distance of the Hungarian border.

Since the end of World War II, Europe had been divided between the post war west and those sealed away behind the Iron Curtain. Poland, Eastern Germany, Czechoslovakia, Hungary, Romania, Bulgaria, and Albania had all ended up on what my 1970s upbringing and education fervently considered to be the *wrong* side.

After the war, the Soviet Union had distanced itself from western influence. There were, of course, all sorts of social and economic impacts to having communism imposed on the citizens of those countries. What it meant to me was that I had a twenty-four-hour visa which restricted me to only being able to transitHungary. From the moment I entered, I had only a single day in which to leave the country and have my exit visa stamped at the distant land border with Yugoslavia. An overnight stop, of any sort, was absolutely forbidden.

I decided that the best course of action for the day would be to ride fairly hard, broadly following the course of the Danube, get past Vienna and then find somewhere to camp. That would leave me within a few tens of miles from the Hungarian border.

There was a buffet continental breakfast set up in the back of the onsite store, so I soon had a helmet full of buns and cheese and had the tent packed and ready to go. The route out of town, back towards the Autobahn, took me back up the steep cobbled street. I admit to having butterflies once more, but the weather was dry, and while it was bumpy, it didn't cause me any of the terrors of the previous night.

Traffic was heavy as I hit the tail end of the commuters vying to navigate their shiny Mercedes-Benz and BMWs to their jobs in Nuremberg.

It is sometimes difficult when riding in Germany to not be constantly reminded by the city and place names of events that happened in World War II. Nuremberg of course became famous after the war. It was the city used to host the Nuremberg trials, the place where German Nazi politicians and military leaders involved in war crimes and crimes against humanity were brought to justice, many of whom were later executed in the same city. I didn't know why Nuremberg was chosen so I looked it up. One reason was the Palace of Justice. The Palace of Justice is a huge and, critically, undamaged by allied bombing courtroom, that already existed there. But the main reason was that Nuremberg had been the location where the Nazi Party's laws stripping Jews of their citizenship and basic human rights were first passed. Fitting then, and hugely symbolic, that it became the place of the subsequent humiliation and demise of that evil regime.

The speed limit around major cities such as Nuremberg is 120 km/h, about 75 mph. But of course, outside of restricted areas, marked by black and white signs, there is no top speed limit on the Autobahn and boy—do some of those folks really make the most of it!

Most sections of the Autobahn are only dual carriageway, so before overtaking you really need to check those rear-view mirrors with a dash of care. On one section near Velburg, I checked my mirrors to make sure the outside lane behind me was clear. There was no sign of traffic all the way back to the distant horizon, so I indicted to pull out to pass a large truck. By the time I got alongside him I glanced back in my mirrors to find a bright orange police Porsche 911 barely three feet from my rear wheel.

He flashed me to get out of his way, which I did as quickly as I safely could, and he roared past me. He then pulled in front of me to let a canary yellow Lamborghini and a Rosso Corsa Ferrari 288 GTO past him. Bear in mind I wasn't hanging about, I was already cruising at around 115 mph. To close on me so quickly the others must have been doing well over 150 mph. The Ferrari driver slowed to pull up alongside me. He checked the bike out and then gave me a cheery grin and a thumbs up and floored it. With a heady V8 burble, he passed the cop and quickly caught up with his buddy in the Lambo, already a bright yellow speck in the distance.

I crossed the Danube for the first time just south of Regensburg, a broad sweep of sparkling, sun-dappled brilliance set amidst gently sloping verdant banks and rows of tall snow-white bullrushes. The Danube is the second longest river in Europe. It is second only to the Volga which is in Russia. I never really considered Russia to be part of Europe so, at least in my estimation, that makes the Danube the longest. The Danube rises in Germany and flows southeast for a startlingly lengthy 1,770 miles, passing through Austria, Slovakia, Hungary, Croatia, Serbia, Romania, Bulgaria, Moldova, and Ukraine before draining into the Black Sea.

I crossed the river four or five more times that afternoon as the sun steadily arced across the clear blue sky. The temperature continued to rise but the big Suzuki just kept burbling easily away.

I stopped only to have my passport stamped at the border with Austria outside the town of Suben, close to the crossing of the river Inn, the same river that would continue to meander splendidly through the Austrian countryside towards the town of Innsbruck far to my south-east.

I passed the city of Linz around lunchtime. Even over the constant whistle of the sound of the wind rushing past my visor and the deep burble of the bike beneath me, I could still hear my stomach rumbling. I saw a sign for the river Enns and pulled off the autobahn to navigate towards the town of the same name to find somewhere pretty I could eat my sandwiches.

I found what I was looking for on the banks of the river, just half a mile south of the town. The river Enns was a broad and sun dappled tributary of the Danube that lay to my north. I listened to the bike pinking and pinging behind me as I made a ham and cheese sandwich and drained a bottle of tepid water seated on the sloping sward of pleasant greenery that led down to the edge of the clear running river.

The rows of ancient cottages behind me glowed the colour of autumn pumpkins. A few cars rattled over the iron bridge to cross the river, but otherwise I was in a quiet idyll. A group of friends paddling red and yellow kayaks made fetching swirls and white tinged eddies in the water as they rowed slowly past me, struggling against the current. One saw me and looked up to raise a hand in greeting. He smiled and shouted something in German which I didn't understand so I just smiled and waved back, shouting "Ja, Ja," and grinned back like an idiot in response.

The church bell rang the hour, and I realised I need to be on the move again.

Back on the road, the countryside was still dominated by rich pasture, crops of corn and rapeseed, dotted with patches of ancient woodland. Low rolling verdant pasture speckled with cottonwool ball sheep lay on either side.

The first peaks of the Alps had finally shown up. I had been scanning the horizon for them for close to an hour. They lay like a line of tiny, jagged incisors across the landscape in the hazy distance. As the Alps made their first appearance, the cottages and houses of the towns that occasionally rose into view almost magically became distinctly Tyrolean, cuckoo clock pretty.

The hills around me grew in stature, clothed in the emerald sheen of the firs, they drew me through a verdant tunnel. I had been on the road for over five hours and was tiring quickly, so was pleased when I picked up the first of the road signs that pointed me towards Vienna.

The weather had been magnificent, clear skies and temperatures in the low eighties. Traffic slowed as I approached Vienna, but the Autobahn gave the city itself a wide looping berth and soon I was through and heading east towards Hungary. I stopped for gas so that I could start the next day with a full tank of fuel. Because I couldn't stop in Hungary, I hadn't brought any Hungarian Forint with me. With a full tank I began to look for a suitable camping site.

I saw a sign for a decent looking place close to the banks of the Danube in a little town called Haslau-Maria Ellend. On the way in I passed a small restaurant at the top of the hill and made a mental note. I had ridden for close to six hours and covered a decent 372 miles. I know that, for those sat in a La-Z-Boy in the USA, reading this with a gun in one hand and a weak domestic beer in the other that 300+ miles is just a golf cart ride to the nearest Walmart, but in Europe it is considered quite the long drive. In a future life I would live in Atlanta and folks from the mid-west and beyond would often remark, "how nice to live so close to the sea." Atlanta's nearest coast is over a four-hour drive away.

The campsite was perfect. There was a gently sloping hill with a clean and well provisioned toilet block at the top. There was a smattering of tourer caravans with the usual mix of Audi and BMW cars parked close by, but I seemed to be the only one with a tent, so I parked up the bike and unpacked. I always carried a plank of wood which I kept under the tent bag on the rear carrier. I put it on the ground and hefted the bike up onto its centre stand, making sure my trusty piece of timber was pinioned underneath. Without it there was always the chance the heavy bike on the steel stand would simply sink into damp grass and topple over.

With tent erected and all my stuff piled inside I changed into a shirt less able to stand up and move around of its own accord, had what we call in the North of England '*a Wigan wash*,' namely a judicious sprinkle of some cold water under each armpit, masked what odour remained with a spray of some Brut aftershave, and walked back up the hill to the restaurant I had passed on the way in.

It was called Das Restaurant Wasserfall, and sure enough a little waterfall lay at the back of the restaurant which babbled and chuckled its way down the hill towards the Danube. I took a table at the window that looked out onto the jagged, mist fronded spread of the Alps that had slowly grown to dominate the skyline. The sun was starting to set in a clear evening sky, setting fire to the tops of the rising peaks. I ordered a large Pfeffer steak with fries and an even larger pilsner.

The steak was immense, grilled to medium-rare perfection and covered in spicy black and red peppercorns. The fries were fresh and crispy and soaked up the meat and pepper juices. The beer was icy cold, frosty, and dry and I almost drained it at first touch. The server was sweet and observant and brought me another as soon as the empty glass touched the table. She could tell I was a man not to be trifled with. Either that or my body odour had repulsed her to such an extent that she wanted to curtail my dining experience as quickly as she could.

As I cradled my full stomach and drank my fill, I pondered what the next day would bring. It would be my first exposure to life behind the Iron Curtain. Hungary was a territory of what I had been taught to fear, the dreaded USSR, the Union of Soviet Socialist Republics.

Only a few weeks before I had set off on the trip, an animated film had been released in the UK. It was called '*When the Wind Blows*,' and told the tale of Jim and Hilda Bloggs and their struggle to survive after a global nuclear strike had been unleashed on Britain by the USSR. In the story, an Intercontinental Ballistic Missile detonates close to their hometown in rural Sussex. The tale is dark and grim, and I hate to tell you that, though I normally relish a good, animated movie, this one does not end well. There is radiation fallout, poisoning and death. It was exceedingly macabre and, given where I was, strangely poignant.

This was the world I had grown up in. The era of the Cold War. A time when mutual nuclear assured destruction seemed shockingly inevitable. We were taught what to do if the sirens and warnings of an imminent nuclear strike were on its way. We were reliably informed we would have just enough time to boil an egg before hiding under a table. Honestly, that, in essence, was the advice and reassurance the government had to offer to its perpetually frightened citizenry.

The message was not about *if* it happened, but rather *when* it would happen, and we were taught to generally fear the Russians and their evil agenda. And tomorrow I would be taking my first peek behind their dreaded curtain. I would be stepping into a world that I had been taught was grey and totalitarian, one where political dissent was met with instant brutality and a one-way trip to the frozen steppes of Siberia to live a life of servitude in the salt mines. I would be visiting a world of fuel shortages, cheap vodka, and communism. One where the proletariat were forced to queue for hours to buy a single wildly sprouting potato.

While I had mused on these unhappy thoughts and sipped my beer, other diners had drifted in, and the babble of foreign voices reached across the restaurant. Oh well, tomorrow I would see the truth for myself. At least I would get to ride through Budapest, just the sound of which sounded incredibly romantic and adventurous in my young mind.

I was deliriously happy and ordered another beer. As I leant back savouring the taste, I saw a few of the diners point out of the window. The word '*föhn*' drifted around the room, picked up and repeated by the other diners, always in whispered tones of awe.

I looked outside to see the peaks of the mountains glowing a luminescent pink. Marshmallow clouds had appeared in a gap between the peaks and were moving in earnest down into the valley. They were quite pretty to watch as they roiled and spread, and I reached into my pocket to get my camera thinking I might take a picture.

The sound of scraping chairs and dropped clanging cutlery made me look back around at the other diners. They were all leaving, hurriedly paying checks, and moving back into the car park. I had almost no German, other than being able to buy anything up to three beers and asking if a double room was available, I was without language to ask, or understand, what was so worrying. But humankind has survived for millennia by acting like sheep, copying the behaviour of others, so I paid my check and joined the exodus.

As I walked slowly back to the campsite, I was still wondering what the fuss was all about. The sun had finally set, and darkness began to steal the definition from the trees and bushes that lined the road, pushed their silhouettes backwards to join the greater shadows beyond.

Suddenly a flashing crackle of lightning turned the night into noon, accompanied by a simultaneous hair raising *CRAAACK* of thunder. Then somebody poured a colossal and endless bucket of icy water on me. It was steady and relentless and in less than a second, I was absolutely soaked. Trees shook, leaves and debris swirled all around me. Lightning forked across the sky and ten million gallons of freezing water was dumped, like a giant emptying his cold bathwater directly onto the top of my head. I had never been quite so wet quite so quickly.

I picked up my pace into a little jog, the beer sloshing from side to side in my bloated stomach. The road had filled with water. Water sloshed over my boots; it ran like a babbling brook down the road in front of me.

As soon as I got back to the campsite, I checked on the bike. I was bent almost double to avoid the worst of the maelstrom. The bike was fine, still standing firm on the plank I had placed it on. I unzipped the tent and crawled inside. The wind was still picking up. I was soaked and freezing.

From inside the tent the sound of the storm was intense, it screamed and howled like a banshee, plucked at the seams of the tent, snapped the fabric, and shook the poles. It lifted the groundsheet like a wild and angry bronco underneath me. Without the visual balance of seeing the trees bend under the gusts, my imagination ran wild, painted giants and beasts rampaging through the campground, tearing the roots from the ground, wailing at the heavens.

The pitch of the storm shifted, a doppler whine, a howl of fury so sudden, the change in air pressure made my ears pop. The tent was whipped wildly backwards and forwards. I was forced to lay face down, spread-eagled, in an attempt to keep the tent from being picked up and hurled into the sky with me inside of it. Then the inevitable, the pegs that faced the barrage were plucked from the ground and the tent collapsed onto me.

For a second all was wild disorientation, pinned beneath the fabric, uncertain even of the orientation of the opening. I grabbed my pocketknife and crawled around the tent feeling my way along the seam until I located the zip at the front. I crawled through the opening, already damp knees instantly sopping on the soaking grass.

Outside was pitch black, I could have been struck blind. The dark sky raced like ravens overhead, and the rain drove in horizontal sheets across the field. The caravans that surrounded me shook and rocked as the wind howled, tore itself into frustrated fragments on their impenetrable facades.

I found the first tent peg at the front corner. I had to put the knife down to grab it. I pulled the drawstring tight and jammed the peg as deep as I could into the ground, angled against the force of the wind. I crawled across the soaked grass to find the next peg, only to find the tent ripped at the other corner and no means to secure the peg. As I scuttled blindly around on the ground I knelt on the open blade of the knife. The tip went deep into my knee, and I let out a yell of pain and frustration. I was cold, soaked to the skin and bleeding. The tent was ripped and impossible to secure in the dark and against this wind.

As I crawled back into the destroyed tent, under the soaked fabric, I looked out across the campground. The caravans were still being buffeted by the wind, but they all had warm glowing lights that peeped from the curtains of cosy bedroom windows. They all looked warm and safe, secured against the elements. I thought about asking for help, to see if the owners would consider letting me sleep on the floor for the night. But in the end, I pulled the door flaps closed, zipped them as best I could and slunk to the back of the tent.

With the damp nylon fabric around my ears and water rolling in icy trickles down my neck, I pulled my drenched sleeping bag around my hunched and trembling shoulders and, exhausted, fell into yet another uneasy slumber.

GULAG

At the arrival of first light the storm and dawn finally broke in unison. For myself, I had broken a little earlier in the night. I had slept only a little, like a cramped airline passenger on a red eye crossing of the Atlantic, I had been buffeted and rocked. My legs were cramped and the damp sleeping bag had ensured that there was no way for me to dry out.

I hobbled on a wounded knee out of the tent with a wide and prolonged yawn and a stretch that cracked my back with a report loud enough to wake the rest of the camp. I stood for a long minute to survey the damage.

Thankfully, the bike was still standing and undamaged. The rest of the campground was a mess. Fallen branches, stripped from the trees lay in tangled heaps. The bins by the toilet block had been lifted, contents emptied and dumped unceremoniously onto the wet grass. One of the caravan owners had neglected to secure his awning and it had torn, one end still secured to the van, the rest of it whipping and snapping like a festival banner in the dying wind.

I pulled out the sleeping bag and spread it across the bike to dry in the warming rays of the rising sun, took some time to examine the tent. It actually wasn't too bad. A few of the tent pegs were bent and had been torn from the ground and scattered, but only a couple of tie out points had been ripped and rendered entirely unusable. I dragged the rest of my stuff out of the tent and lay it all on the grass to dry while I rolled up and folded the tent and packed the poles and pegs.

I finally had time to look at the cut my own knife had made in my knee. It was a nasty wound, deep, jagged, and still bleeding profusely. I got out my first aid kit, took the tube of TCP antiseptic cream and with a trembling finger pushed the unguent as far as I was able into the open wound. I put a couple of sticking plasters across each other in a crisscross, like those you see on the hairy bums of cartoon characters and hoped it wouldn't get infected.

I didn't have much time to wait for my gear to dry. I needed to leave Austria soon. The border with Hungary lay only twenty-five miles away, close to the town of Neue Teilung. I then needed to ride across Hungary in time to exit and safely enter Yugoslavia. It was only a little more than a 300-mile ride, but I had two border crossings and a ride through the bustling city of Budapest to negotiate. It was also difficult to ascertain what else I might have to contend with. Information was scarce in those days. There were few written guides available for the western traveller, and while Tim Berners-Lee and some geeky, bearded friends had managed to connect a few early computers together to send the first nudes to each other, the concept of the internet as the world wide web of today was a very distant dream.

I was damp all over, but the sun was racing into the sky, and I figured that a quick blast on the Autobahn should air everything out nicely, so I packed the bike, checked the map, and hit the road. It was only a few short miles before traffic first petered out and then what little remained began to slow as we approached the border with Hungary.

Tall guard towers rose to dominate the horizon, like sentries on stilted iron legs, sketched directly from the mind of H. G. Wells they strode with purpose across the foreign landscape. Tall fencing, topped with razor-wire ran alongside the road for as far as the eye could see. On one side, the West. On the other, communism and the start of the East. The unknowable might of the USSR. At the time the largest country on earth.

I pulled up in the queue and waited my turn to have my paperwork inspected when the boy with the scar shaped like a question approached me. Five minutes later, and strongly motivated by the muzzle of the submachine gun I was walking, stiff-legged, with a belly full of dread, across to the low concrete building with the green painted corrugated steel roof.

My heartbeat too fast and suddenly I was desperately thirsty, my throat a Saharan sandstorm. The exterior of the building was entirely utilitarian, not a single adornment or pretence at architecture. A tall pile of breeze blocks with a row of high, barred windows, and a single steel door. I was ushered inside and looked back just in time to see a chink of hopeful sunlight squeezed into oblivion as the door clanged, like a sprung steel bear trap, shut behind me.

The interior mirrored the exterior. Something erected in haste to fulfil a function. A processing plant; my first taste of communist austerity. A row of cubicles ran around the wall to the left and in the centre were steel tables and chairs. The high windows threw little light across the room. The air in the room captured the essence of tedium and fear. Dust motes swirled in blue cigarette smoke. Soldiers waited, wreathed in the clouds of their own exhalations. They sat, slumped, unkempt in tattered uniforms, bored by their duties they glanced across at me.

Hard eyes followed the squeaked sounds of my motorcycle boots on the cheap linoleum floor, across to the cubicle where I was ushered to sit by question Mark. The cubicle was sparse, painted the colour of rust. The chair was steel, angular, and intentionally uncomfortable. A dark brown A4 ring binder was propped up on the table, it was stuffed, crammed with dog eared formal looking documents. A framed picture of Mikhail Gorbachev was pinned at an annoyingly wonky angle to the wall. His port-wine stain birthmark had been badly doctored with a biro to crudely resemble a cock and balls. An ash tray piled high, spilled its foul-smelling contents onto the table.

The top of the polished steel table in front of me was dented and scratched. I looked down at my hands that rested there. In between my trembling fingers I saw a face. Strangely familiar but pale and frightened, distorted by the warped surface. The face was mine, but at the same time not. My thoughts reached out to home and my Mum's kitchen table, and I wondered if she was OK and was, she, in turn, thinking of me.

Mark took my passport and walked across to one of the officials. The man was marked as the commander by the vermillion satin band that ran around the middle of his jaunty peaked cap. He had his heavy boots on the steel table and a coarse shadow of stubble across his cheeks, a burning ember of a hand rolled cigarette in the corner of his mouth. I could see them talking as he thumbed through my passport. Mark pointed to a page and the grizzled official shook his head and pointed across the room to a heavy steel door that looked disturbingly like a cell. My heart sank even as it beat out a funeral march. Question Mark nodded understanding and returned to my little cubicle. He motioned me to stand with the muzzle of the gun. Suddenly, I was loathe to leave. The cubicle seemed to suddenly be safe, a comfortable and familiar haven in the sudden heaving tempest that had become my morning.

But Mark was not to be denied. I stood on shaky legs to be cajoled across the room towards the threatening steel door. He knocked with a closed fist, and we waited. Nothing happened so he knocked again, this time with the stock of his weapon. The sound boomed across the office space prompting one of the officials to hurl a string of abuse.

Finally, a thin wiry man opened the door and scowled us inside. The room was dark and small. A single steel chair, the same uncomfortable model as the ones in the cubicle, had been intentionally positioned in the dead centre of the room. By the wall, facing it, was some equipment. My mind raced down dark avenues, explored all possibilities of what this strange room might represent. Unfortunately, each desperate avenue was a cul-de-sac. The dentistry scene from the movie Marathon Man began to play in the darkest echelons of my wild imagination. Torture and interrogation seemed inevitable. And what then? A gulag, breaking rocks in a salt mine, struggling to hold my sledgehammer with Siberia cold hands and missing fingernails.

Mark left without a word and the door closed behind me. Wiry guy motioned me to towards the chair and as I stumbled across, mind numb and defeated, he turned on a light to reveal a camera and angled flash gun all set atop a tripod.

Ten minutes later, I was stood once more beside my bike, blinking in the sunshine I had been certain I would never see again. I looked down at my shaking hands to see the new photo of me inserted into the now stamped visa in my passport. The face was mine, but haunted, hollow-eyed, and ashen.

Budapest

After crossing into Hungary, I rode far too hard and much too fast for a solid hour. My feelings were a competing gordian knot, a jangling confusing mess of threads impossible to unpick. Alternating waves of anger, humiliation, relief and the residue of fear and despair broke over me. I needed to drain the leftover adrenalin from my system, stop my hands from shaking on the handlebars.

My first taste of communism had reinforced every preconception and stereotype I had been taught to expect. I had wilfully entered a grim and austere place. A dangerous and wickedly unfathomable contradiction. And I was entirely alone.

But as I pulled the land under me, mile by mile, my clothing slowly dried in the warm summer sunshine. The fields were broad, verdant, rolling, and pleasant. Lines of tall poplars and ash reached into the empty sky, they calmed my mind. The landscape was the antithesis of the grey bunkers and monochrome hues I had been expecting.

I thought more about the strange, threatening incident at the border. I didn't know at the time, if the entire debacle had been a joke to amuse the guards, or just a casual carelessness, a symptom of those cold war days. I suspected the latter, but I was happy to be free and, on my way again, this time with the correct photo attached to the visa. Slowly, my jangling nerves subsided, the fear leached away. I was very young and quick to forget and still keen to see this hidden country.

The foothills of the alps gradually subsided into an undulating patchwork of distant hills. I was riding due east, away from the gravity of the alps, and bound for Budapest.

Buda and Pest were originally two different cities that spanned the mighty Danube. Together they created a twin city, each distinct but linked by history and hedonism. Buda's hills sit on the west bank facing the flat expanse of Pest across the wide expanse of the river that has brought its occupants wealth from the Black Sea to the east and

Europe to the west for a thousand years. There are seven major bridges across the Danube, that link the two halves, create a single thriving eco-system of population, culture, and commerce.

The seven bridges are named, from north to south, the Árpád Bridge, the Margaret bridge, the Széchenyi Chain Bridge, the Elizabeth bridge, the Liberty bridge, the Petőfi Bridge and the Rákóczi Bridge.

It was across all of these that I now found myself unintentionally, and repeatedly crisscrossing the Danube in the noon heat of the day. I started this maddening hour of trying to escape the city on the beautiful Széchenyi Chain Bridge. I crossed from west to east, as planned, marvelling at the breadth of the Danube there. Slow and shallow, dotted with tacking, seabird white sailboats and tar-black smoking steamers, it snaked and wound its way unhurriedly through the heart of the steaming city.

I happily began to navigate my way through the elegant suburbs only to find myself looking back at the Széchenyi bridge, but now from the south, on the Elizabeth bridge, as I crossed the Danube once more, from Pest, back into Buda.

Inside my increasingly fetid motorcycle helmet I tutted and smiled at my foolish navigational faux pas. The day was stifling, and I cracked the visor, as traffic slowed, to let in some air. I navigated through a couple of right turns to make my way back to the Széchenyi bridge only to now see it from the north looking back down the Danube from the Margaret bridge. No big deal, still heading east I just need to find a way back to the main road out of the city and then begin my journey south towards Yugoslavia.

Now on back roads, I passed through a market area that overflowed with life. All of its brilliant, jarring colours, sweet spice fragrances, nose-wrinkling stenches, shouts, screams and contagious laughter reached out to me. Stall holders with walnut sun-wrinkled skin, rheumy eyes brimming with wisdom, peeped from beneath bushy greying brows. The market vendors watched in awe as the big Suzuki burbled through their crowded streets, a big Japanese motorcycle, incongruous in that setting, an exceedingly rare sight in those turbulent political times.

I was an interloper from the west. An intruder in their midst. I wouldn't have attracted more attention if I had been beamed down to appear out of thin air amongst them.

I was hungry and the scent of hot grease caught my attention. A man, crooked and white-haired, dressed in what appeared to be a striped burlap sack was tossing lamb, peppers, and onions into a huge, blackened pan over a crackling open flame and shovelling the heady mix into freshly charred pita breads, handed to him by his equally crooked wife. She, in turn, sprinkled each one with shredded cheese and glistening, juicy pomegranates. Bereft of my usual helmet breakfast, my stomach churned and growled.

I nodded at some play-grimed children who ran alongside me laughing and miming for me to go faster. They all looked identical to me, boys, and girls alike. Raven hair, cut under a bowl by an angry mother with blunt kitchen scissors, dark almond eyes, and wide, white smiles, entirely innocent of the cold war and politics that raged around the borders of their homeland. I blipped the throttle and popped a small wheelie, and they screamed in delight. I smiled to myself and then cursed out loud as the bloody Danube once more hove into sight. Too late to stop and turn around, I inadvertently crossed the Petőfi bridge, back into Buda.

For the next thirty minutes or so I acted like some unwitting participant in a badly written French farce. Back and forth I crossed the Danube. East to west, west to east and back again. At one point I swore I saw myself on the bridge just upstream, going in the opposite direction. No longer did I admire her stately flow. The bloody river could just fuck off for all I cared. Budapest was like some gargantuan black hole of attraction; I was entirely unable to escape its gravity-well pull.

Inside my tank bag the bomb of my soon to expire visa was relentlessly ticking away the seconds and minutes. I wasn't sure what would happen if I got delayed to the point that it actually expired, but I was desperately unwilling to find out. I knew that I did not want to go through another experience like the one I had undertaken to enter the country.

Finally, back where I first started, on the Széchenyi bridge, on the path of my original crossing, I realized where I had first gone wrong. As I crossed the river, the road went up an incline between a claustrophobic press of three-story homes that crowded the street. Ahead of me the road forked, one road to the left and another to the right. But this time I saw that where both big blue road signs displayed an arrow for the inescapable Budapest, only one, a much smaller sign, white and outlined in black, read '*Szeged*' my last destination, a couple of hundred miles south that would lead me to the border with Yugoslavia. I was free!

What little I could see of the city looked elegant and breath-taking. It was a genuine shame that I didn't have time to stop, to explore the streets, and revisit the market to eat one of the greasy lamb pittas, the scent of which still made my stomach complain loudly.

The city was founded two-thousand years ago by the Celts and then subsequently occupied by the Romans. Nowadays, since the collapse of the Iron Curtain, it is besieged by Europeans on hen and stag weekends intent on ignoring its two-millennia of history, culture, and architecture and, instead, they walk around its many bars, wearing strap-on cocks and fannies and getting absolutely shit faced.

As I headed south, the landscape shifted once more. I had entered the Pannonian Basin, once a vast inland sea that existed between the Carpathian Mountains to the west and the Transylvanian Plateau to the east and north. The Pannonian Sea dried up in the Pliocene era, over 2.5 million years ago. While I am sure it had been geographically cataclysmic at the time, and it all sounded enthralling, unfortunately, what it left behind was mind numbingly dull for as far as the eye could see. I had seen more bumps on a flat earth society map. I thought for a moment I had wandered into North Dakota or the Norfolk Broads.

The ride was tedious, and the heat of the day was intense. I had lost time during my temporary incarceration at the border crossing, and more time on the bridges of Budapest. For most of the time on the road I was alone.

There were very few private cars around compared to the busy roads of western Europe.

Close to the border and around Budapest I had seen a smattering of German cars, but this far south the only cars on the roads were of dubious eastern European origin. I didn't recognize a single one, although the manufactures names conjured up images of Red Square, vodka and furry hats. The Volga, Wartburg, Tatra, Polski, ZiL, and of course the Lada, the Škoda and the Trabant, which were soon to become available in the rest of the continent, to the amusement and general disdain of European car lovers.

I whizzed past a tiny Trabant the colour of an anaemic turd. Its two-stroke engine propelled it along at the speed of snail. It appeared to be struggling to overcome even the scant friction of its narrow tires on the tarmac and the prevailing breeze that confronted it. Its occupants were forced to sit so close together that they were clearly in a sexual relationship even if they weren't yet aware of the fact. The young chap who was driving turned the steering wheel left and right in a constant motion, even though we were travelling on a road as straight as a die. I wasn't convinced that the steering wheel in his busy hands was actively attached to the wheels in anything more than a spiritual sense.

His tiny car had been manufactured in Eastern Germany, behind the Berlin Wall and was of such astoundingly poor quality, that when they first became available to the west, the Germans jokingly referred to them as '*Rennpappes,' or Racing Cardboards.* The rumour soon started that they were, in fact, actually made from cardboard which was almost true; they were actually made from a product called Duroplast, a composite of recycled materials.

Between 1957 and 1991, the German Democratic Republic produced a staggering 3.7 million Trabants. However, due to the poor economy and lack of materials, the wait time for the four-passenger vehicle was fourteen years. Fourteen years! The lad I had just passed must have placed the order for his at the font.

When the Berlin wall was brought down in 1989, many Eastern Europeans drove their Trabants west, only to realize that the western alternatives were more economical, offered far greater performance and were of much better quality. They were largely abandoned by the roadside and the Trabant factory was closed only two years later.

The only other traffic were long convoys of heavy articulated lorries. The emission restrictions in the Eastern Bloc were far laxer than in the west and as I passed them, I became enveloped in a choking diesel miasma that clouded my vision and made my eyes stream. The toxic fog became strung out behind me like coal fired airplane contrails.

Finally, hot, and sweaty, I saw a row of red taillights in front of me. I was approaching the town of Szeged which marked the border between Hungary and Yugoslavia. It was a short queue, and it wasn't long before the border guard on the Hungarian side had my passport in his hands. He leafed through the pages with a bored, jaundiced expression until he found the visa. He glanced up at me for a second, but I had my full-face helmet on so he couldn't really see if my face matched that of the photo anyway. He didn't seem to care. He scribbled something across the florid visa, stamped the date and time of my exit and handed it back to me without even looking in my direction. So much for all the hassle I had to endure to enter the bloody place. I rode the hundred yards to the Yugoslavian side with my passport in hand, but the guard there just waved me through, unchallenged into his quietly turbulent country.

A Slavic Argument

I crossed my old friend the Danube close to what my English map told me was the town of Kovilj. The sign itself was entirely unintelligible. The major language here was Serbo-Croatian, although Slovene and Macedonian were also spoken. The alphabet was Cyrillic. In the 1980s, visitors and travellers from the west were extremely limited so no attempt at translation was made. I was having to guess most of the time where in the world I was by comparing the western names on my printed English map with the scramble of unfamiliar letters on the road signs.

The width of the Danube had more than doubled as I had ridden south from Budapest. I crossed on the Viadukt Beška, the longest crossing of the Danube at over 2km in length. As I reached the other side, I started looking for camping sites but there didn't seem to be any type organized camping anywhere. As usual, instead of just dreaming up a destination, packing a tent and setting off, I should have done more research.

Yugoslavia was about to go through a major upheaval in a country that, unknown to ignorant twenty-year-old me, had never stopped going through major upheavals. If, back in the UK, I had spent a little time in the library, actually learning about the countries I was about to travel through, instead of drinking beer and chasing girls, I wouldn't have been as surprised, that some of the countries recent troubles had somewhat negatively impacted the breadth and depth of its tourism industry.

The country of Yugoslavia had been created shortly after the first world war. The country had formerly been a loose grouping of territories that existed as part of the Ottoman Empire and Austria-Hungary. Its first given name was '*Kingdom of Serbs, Croats and Slovenes*' but everybody just called it Yugoslavia. Yugoslavia literally meant '*land of the Slavs*'. It became the '*Kingdom of Yugoslavia*' on the 3rd of October 1929, and then the shit really hit the fan when the Kingdom was invaded by the Axis powers on the 6th of April 1941. During this time, genocide and other atrocities were committed against the Serbs. The

Serb Chetniks, in turn, committed mass crimes against the Muslims and the Croats.

At the end of World War II, the monarchy was abolished, and in 1945 Yugoslavia was renamed the Federal People's Republic of Yugoslavia later that year, when a communist government was established under the rule of one Josip Broz Tito. Tito ruled the country as president until his death in 1980, only six years before my visit. Many described him as a brutal dictator, but the reality was that when Tito died, his guiding stability of the last twenty-seven years was lost, and the movement towards Nationalism began to rise.

The alliance between the republics that made up the Republic of Yugoslavia; Bosnia and Herzegovina, Croatia, Macedonia, Montenegro, Serbia, and Slovenia had always been an uneasy one and ethnic animosity had always festered there, never too far, barely a fingernail scratch from the surface.

Of course, all of this was unknown to naive young me. GCSE History at my state secondary school had barely got around to covering World War II, never mind the nuanced roiling bitter friction between the Serbs, the Montenegrins, the Croats and the Slovenes. I was entirely oblivious of both where I was, and through what epoch of Yugoslavia's shifting history I now rode.

All I was aware of was that a sweet little campground with a shower block and a well provisioned café seemed to be denied to me. I was never averse to adventure. I just liked a cold bottle of beer and a flushing toilet waiting for me at the end of the day. But in rural Yugoslavia, back in that era, there were no hotels or campsites for the few travellers who had made it through the Iron curtain.

Reluctantly, I began to look for a field in which I could pitch my tent. I found what I was looking for in a broad sweeping bend of pasture close to the Danube. On the opposite side of the road, perhaps a mile further on, was a low dark painted building. Outside, a small red sign swung lazily in the warm breeze. I was hopeful that the sign might indicate that the building would be a restaurant or a bar. That was the only incentive I needed. I rolled over the low kerb and parked the bike on its plank, in the pleasing, dappled shade of a spreading ash tree on a flat piece of ground, thirty yards from the river.

The day was glorious, hot as hades, and the sun was still high in the sky, so I took time to spread all of my damp belongings out in the daisy speckled meadow. I changed the dressing on my knee, filled the wound with more TCP cream and put on fresh plasters. My knee had bled steadily throughout the day, but it seemed to be scabbing over nicely. Despite my emergency ministrations making the damage look like something a five-year-old playing doctors and nurses had fixed, I was happy that it wasn't as serious as I thought it might be.

I walked down to the river and watched long painted barges be pulled along by the slow current that led towards the Black Sea far to my east. They were not unlike the barges from home, colourful and hand-painted, piloted by dark skinned, black wool cap wearing sailors, caps pulled down low across hooded eyes. Romany perhaps, the water equivalent of the gypsy caravans this part of the world was infamous for.

The sun was beginning to dip to graze the uppermost leaves of the trees, it sent flickering, dazzling motes of light through their outstretched fingers to blind my eyes. I walked up the meadow and happily found all my stuff to be both still there and mostly bone dry. I put up the tent and made a couple of hasty repairs with some string and gaffer tape and walked back to the road to see if the building I had spotted actually sold food of any sort.

I wasn't entirely sure where I was, so I was pleasantly surprised when I got back to the road to see a sign that had a scrawl of Cyrillic letters — I looked at it sideways and then squinted through my fingers. I took a little liberty with the translation and convinced myself that the sign pointed to the town of Novi Banovci. If so, it meant that I was only twenty miles north of Belgrade. That would put me in a decent place for my ride south tomorrow.

To get to Turkey, and then onward to my final goal of Istanbul, I had to ride across Bulgaria. Unfortunately, Bulgaria was also part of the USSR at the time. Another part of the Iron Curtain to peek behind, and because of that it had a similarly restrictive visa requirement as Hungary. I had to be in, and out of the country within twenty-four-hours. As I walked, I counted the days on my fingers. If I could ride through most of Yugoslavia tomorrow, I could stop close to its border with Bulgaria. Then, the next day, I could cross into Bulgaria in the morning and ride hard to enter Turkey in the late afternoon of the following day. That would place me within sprinting distance of the great city that spanned two continents. It made me smile to myself.

I was alone in a country I didn't understand. Only that morning I had thought I had been arrested and due for a spot of amateur, if enthusiastic dentistry, followed by a stint of hard labour on the Russian Steppes, and now here I was within a two-day ride of Byzantium and Asia. I was young and untroubled, a literal innocent abroad.

My distracted mind had been full of planning, and as I wandered up to the door of the building, I looked up to properly take stock of my surroundings. The building was a long shed or cabin partly secreted in a gap between the trees. On my ten-minute walk from my little camping place not a single car had passed me. No vehicles were parked outside, and I began to think that I had made a mistake. But the sign still swung outside. I couldn't read the letters but on the red piece of clapboard somebody, without skill, had drawn the face of a smiling pig holding a fork. The universal sign for food.

The building had been hastily constructed of planks, erected vertically and all painted black. The paint was peeling in long tendrils that hung, curled like ugly petals against the boards. Rusty nails hung out of the splintered planks like crooked rows of English teeth. There was a row of dusty windows that admitted no view, so I opened the door with a screech of unoiled hinges and stepped inside.

The light from the door sent something scuttling across the floor to disappear beneath a scattering of cheap trestle tables and steel chairs. A blanket of acrid cigarette smoke hung dense and cooling in the air. The smell of burnt grease and old onions tainted the air. A flickering naked bulb was hung from a worn flex that screamed electrocution, it swung lazily and illuminated a bright ring on the nicotine brown ceiling above.

Seated at the tables, the source of the smoke, were five men. They all looked around when I entered. Broad Slavic faces, moustaches that would have shamed Sam Elliot and eyes coloured hard as flint. They were dressed like the bargemen, wool caps bundled onto the table between them, shaved stubble heads revealed. A crowd of amber beer bottles stood to attention. It was clear that I had interrupted their conversation.

Suddenly embarrassed by the unexpected attention I grinned and gave a goofy and extremely gay looking two-handed wave, which they all ignored. But seemingly reassured that the awkward stranger posed absolutely zero threat, they turned to lean back into their conversation. At the back of the little cabin, past the group of men was a bar and behind that, with his back to me, was the largest man I had ever seen. To approach the giant at the bar I had to squeeze past the bargemen, muttering quietly, "excuse me, sorry, sorry," in a very English way as I did so.

Their conversation had changed pitch as I pushed through, but they were so intent upon what seemed to fast becoming an argument that they either didn't notice me, or deemed me so insignificant that they simply ignored my presence. As I approached the bar a voice was raised. The word "Tito," was shouted and a fist thumped down hard on the top of the table which made both myself and the beer bottles jump. Every red-blooded Englishman would have been proud of the manner in which I studiously ignored the increasingly heated fracas.

Somewhat safely at the bar I gave a polite cough, the international noise of "excuse me." The giant ignored me, and I spoke not a word of Serbo-Croatian, Slovene or Macedonian.

"Excuse me," I said, delivered in a much deeper tone than was my norm. The testosterone in the room was reaching a critical level and I felt compelled to compete even as I realized I would not be a player in this field.

The giant shuffled slowly around to face me. His shoulders filled the bar, spread from wall to window like a cormorant's wingspan. I was forced to crick my neck to look up into his face, seven feet tall for certain. He shared the brow and broad nose of his compatriots but was without the moustache. His cheeks were ruddy and his hair, a curly mop, sat like a raven crown on his head. Long tangled sideburns curled towards his broad and gammon shaped mouth, a veritable and impressively intimidating Slavic version of André the Giant.

"Šta?" he muttered, a voice that rose gradually from his toes to boom from his meaty lips.

"Food? Drink?" I asked, miming putting things into my mouth and swallowing an imaginary coke.

"Ah. Hrana?" He pointed to a chalkboard behind him that was so ancient it might have been used for the first, rough draft of the Ten Commandments before they were chiselled into stone. Cyrillic letters were etched onto the faded black, a puzzle of unfamiliar vowels and consonants. It was ridiculous, rendered an infant, I could neither read nor write. I studied the board, literally scratching my head when I noticed, beside one garbled scrawl of unfamiliar letters the giant had helpfully drawn something. Not well unfortunately, but it was the best I had to go on. The crude sketch looked like two domes, one on top of the other with something sandwiched between. That was all the clue I needed, it was a sandwich of some sort, and if I was correct, it was a hamburger.

I leaned across the counter and pointed to the picture. The man mountain followed my gesture and said, "ah hamburger," as his huge finger squirmed inside his ear to unblock and remove a piece of wax the size of a pound of Cheddar. I fervently began to hope that the burger came without toppings.

"Yes!" I said. The Russian word sprang into my head; how different could it be? In triumph, "Da!"

"Da...HAMBURGER," he bellowed into the back of the cabin, where the head chef of this esteemed establishment must have resided, all said as he wiped the wax from his finger onto the front of his shirt. I tried not to let my curling lip of distaste be too obvious, but the noise from the bargemen interrupted us. I turned to see that the conversation had tilted into a full argument.

A chair was pushed back, a man stood, another shouted and pointed. I heard Tito's name called several times; harsh voices were raised into furious anger. Beer bottles rolled on the table and the man nearest me reached for one.

Perfect. Now here I was stranded, waiting for my hamburger, stuck between André the fucking giant's bigger brother, and five furious bare-knuckle gypsy fighters. There was absolutely no way I could get through the feuding men and back to the exit. I pushed my back up against the bar as one of the men poked the bigger of the men in the chest. The big man shoved the smaller guy and the man holding the bottle broke it on the table and stepped in to wave the jagged edges of what remained under the big man's chin. Voices were raised and I became certain that here, in the middle of absolutely bum fuck nowhere, I would meet a greasy end in the middle of a brawl I didn't even understand, my pale body bundled unceremoniously into the woods for the wild boar to find.

I let out a low moan of despair when the giant tapped me on the shoulder and pushed a heavy paper bag, the burger I assumed, cooked suspiciously quickly into my hands.

"Idi," he rumbled pointing through a door into the kitchen area. I walked hastily through to find a small raisin faced woman bent over a griddle. She smiled at me and muttered something. It might have been "for the love of God, call the police and free me from the hell of this pitiful existence," but I would never find out. A door lay open, one that led back to the pasture and my little tent. I nodded in mute pity at her situation and fled.

I jogged back down the road and when I got back to the tent, I opened the bag to find a beefburger, juicy and bloody, like you find on much of the continent, and a cold bottle of beer. The beer was labelled 'LAV 7' and tasted delicious. It was strong, crisp, and hoppy, cold and refreshing. I wiped the grease from my chin, glugged the beer and reflected on the ugly scene in the scruffy bar. I thought it a shame. I had only just arrived, and the countryside so far was spectacular. But the argument and the fight seemed to perfectly capture the essential zeitgeist of Yugoslavia in that snapshot of a moment in time.

Still, overall, I was content with the day. In those younger days, that's all it took—a full belly and a fizzy head. I rolled into my dry sleeping bag with a burp so loud and prolonged that it startled the herons on the river into noisy flight.

Dead Horses and Tortoises

I awoke to a dazzling day. A day that all riders of motorcycles dream of. Especially ones who have hailed from Britain's drippy shores.

The sun was already rising above the treetops and the road was a series of fast winding curves that, for the first twenty miles or so, followed the course of the Danube. The tarmac was smooth and traffic mostly non-existent. The note from the exhaust was a deep burble of power, the bike alive under me. The needle on the tacho flickered in response to the throttle, the gears were slick and the tires sticky. The sun through the trees lay in dapples across the road in front of me. The bumbling Trabants and Skodas were few and easy to pick off on the big Suzuki,

I carved past them with ease. The wind was warm and sky clear—it was a beautiful day to be on a bike, on the open road, heading from somewhere scary to somewhere possibly even scarier. Somewhere I had never been before. One of life's true pleasures.

I passed the outskirts of Belgrade and took the opportunity to stop for gas. The petrol station sold basic groceries, so I bought some packaged ham and cheese and some bread with my Yugoslavian dinars. South of Belgrade I parted ways with the Danube for the last time. She would continue almost due east to stretch across the plains of nearby Romania, home of the Draculas, to form part of its northern border with Bulgaria. My path lay to the south.

Getting gas and food when I did turned out to be good timing. The further I rode from Belgrade the more rustic the roads and the infrastructure became. The wide road narrowed, and the tarmac became a combination of pot-holed and treacherously smooth, the gravel worn entirely away. I was in the first foothills of the vast Balkan Mountain range that lay to my east. Each town I passed through became smaller than the last until they dwindled into small villages and hamlets, a handful of small leaning cottages clustered around the road that cut through them.

The ride was like sitting astride a time machine, a two-wheeled DeLorean. The further and faster I rode, the flux-capacitor took me further and further back in time. Cars petered out, replaced by carts pulled by horses. I stopped at midday in a small and entirely unpronounceable village. I parked the bike and cobbled together something that resembled a sandwich, seated on the grass by the side of the road. The few cottages were made of stone, small with pitched tiled roofs. A girl walked by. She wore brightly coloured knee socks and an embroidered skirt, and an apron embroidered with bright red peonies. Over the shirt she wore a traditional jelek, a brightly coloured, short waistcoat. I was astounded to see that across her young shoulders she bore an old wooden yoke with twin tin buckets of milk balanced on either end. I looked further down the road to see if she was part of a traditional festival, but she was alone, performing her daily chores, dressed in the exact same garb as her byzantine ancestors.

I was truly shocked at first, but as the day continued the sight became common. Outside of the major towns and cities, rural Yugoslavia had been lost in time. Men wearing Šajkača caps with embroidered waistcoats and coarse woollen trousers tied tight above their leather and horn toed Opanci shoes. The women were dressed like my milkmaid, garbed in delicately embroidered aprons, and pleated skirts, all performing chores with hand tools and horses. The rooftops of the homes were naked, not a power line or a TV aerial in sight. Outside of the major metropolitan centres, the 20th, and perhaps even the 19th century had simply left the smaller villages in their wake.

Back on the road the Balkan Mountains had added their bulk to my journey. The road was still narrow and poorly maintained but it climbed steadily, a series of twisting, and turning hairpins that pulled me up towards the peaks. The sides of the cliffs crumbled where stormwater had scored the mountainside, and tumbled firs lay amid the bracken of the dense forests. Towering cliffs of blue granite rose above the skyline.

The afternoon was waning, and I needed to start to think of finding a place to stop. I passed a sign for a village. The sign bore the usual scribble of unfamiliar letters, but the initial letter looked like a letter 'M' but one drawn by a pissed toddler so, based on where I thought I should be, I thought it might be the Moklište on my map.

There was literally nothing there, not a sign of a single residence. I rounded a tight right-hand bend and there, to my eternal surprise, by the side of the road lay a huge dead horse. I didn't recognize it for what it was at first glance. It had succumbed to whatever ill had felled it by falling and rolling onto its back. Its stiff legs were extended into the air like some oversized and upended dining room table. Its lips were pulled back over large yellow incisors, a rictus grin below eyes unsighted by the crows. The buzz of the hungry flies was loud even over the noise of the engine.

This ghoulish vision transfixed me. I craned my neck even as I hurtled past to keep it in view. I looked back to the road with a shake of the head and ran straight over a huge tortoise that was making its way, far too slowly, across the road. It was like hitting a giant boulder. Suddenly I was Evel Knievel. The bike flew into the air and landed with a sickening crunch, handlebars flapping violently from side to side. I slowly twisted the throttle and the bike eventually settled and came out of the 'tank-slapper.'

I pulled over as quickly as I could to the side of the road, breathing hard, and walked back to see if the tortoise was injured. It was. It was a ghastly sight. The shell had cracked open, and the force of the heavy bike had clamped down on what remained of the shell to sever the creature's head and legs like a giant pastry cutter. There was nothing I could do for the poor thing, and the stench from Seabiscuit in the corner there, was nauseating. I walked back to the bike to find that the hard landing had cracked open the exhaust pipe that lay slung low under the bike. Damn it!

The bike still ran just fine but the noise was dreadful. It had been loud before but now it physically hurt. It sounded just like two skeletons perpetually fucking on top of a tin roof in a thunderstorm. It made my ears hurt and my head ache.

According to my map there was a major town coming up. A chance to refuel and try to find somewhere to stay for the night. I knew I was close to the border with Bulgaria, ideal for my early start tomorrow. If I was where I thought I might be, I was close to the town of Pirot, only fifteen miles or so from the border with Bulgaria.

The town was a decent size. It had places that I thought might be factories and rows of buildings that might be houses, but it was a bit strange. Sometimes when you ride through towns in southern Germany or Austria or France, you come upon a place and you think, this could be in England. The architecture is different, and you are obviously riding on the wrong side of the road. And it is sunny of course. But it isn't all completely alien. The basic functions of the buildings are familiar at least. Not so in Yugoslavia. A place I thought might be a school turned out to be a crematorium and a building I thought might be a supermarket was actually a gaudy nursing home.

The one building I did thankfully recognise, as I watched my fuel needle dip into the red, was a brightly painted EKO petrol station. I pulled in and blipped the throttle as I pulled up to the pump. The bike was so loud, the attendant immediately came out with a worried expression on his face, expecting to see a Harrier jet performing a vertical landing on his forecourt. I waved him away with a hand of reassurance and refuelled the Suzuki in the baking heat of the late afternoon.

When I finally went inside to pay, the attendant didn't speak a single word of English so all of my questions about hotels and campsites fell on unknowing ears. I rode another mile or so south and with no better options in sight, and the border with Bulgaria looming, I just pulled off the road and parked the bike on my little plank of wood in the forest. I pitched the tent and made another sandwich and sat watching darkness creep across the landscape, to steal the detail from the trees, fade the green to black, all the time listening for the cry of the grey wolves that roamed these hills and hoping that it was too hot for bears and too far a flight path for the fangy, flappy things that lived in nearby Transylvania.

Tractor Tires

I slept incredibly well. I think the challenge and fatigue of the last few days had finally caught up with me. I had eaten all of the bread, cheese and meat for dinner the previous night and was unlikely to find anywhere in Bulgaria to stock up, so, even though it was perhaps a somewhat incongruous choice for breakfast, I took some time to heat the Billy can over my little gas burner and made myself a chicken and mushroom pot noodle and an instant coffee. For my North American readers, think cheap Ramen noodles but with a dash of flavour. With my belly full of re-hydrated brown chicken lumps and miniscule pieces of mushroom that coated the tongue and tasted of Papier-mâché, I dug myself a private little hole in the woods and got ready to depart.

With everything packed I hit the road and soon I was in the short queue just outside the town of Gradinje to cross into Bulgaria. Another country held firmly behind the Iron Curtain, today would be a semi-wasted day spent in transit. No opportunity to sightsee or explore, I had to be in Turkey by the end of the day which meant at the very least a solid five-hour ride. The cracked exhaust caught the attention of everybody in the queue including the armed guards, but, unlike the Hungarian militia, the Bulgarians were amicable and interested, they clamoured around me pointing and jabbering away, intrigued by the bike.

I admit to being a tad nervous when I presented my visa and passport. The guard asked me to remove my helmet, double checked that my dishevelled appearance at least somewhat resembled the photograph and proceeded to wave me through without any fuss.

I was torn by leaving Yugoslavia. The scenery had been spectacular, towering cliffs, lush meadows, decent roads. But so isolated by the years of Tito's presidency. It felt like a country with a chance to rise from its self-imposed shackles. To shrug off the constraints of communism and let its people breathe. But it was clear from the little I had experienced that Tito's towering shadow might not be so easy to cast aside. I would see more and have the opportunity to spend some time on the western coast on the ride home in a few days.

As I entered Bulgaria, a sky the colour of periwinkle petals streaked with cirrostratus clouds lay strung out high in the atmosphere. Blankets of corn and rape fields lay on either side of the road. The air was heavily scented with barley and summer. I could have heard the buzz of insects beyond number had it not been for the cracked exhaust pipe that assaulted my ears, mile after bloody mile.

Long rows of barbed wire fences lay on either side of the road. Every thirty yards or so a sign was secured to the fence with wire ties. The signs, as usual, were indecipherable, but luckily for me, underneath the Cyrillic was a picture of a camera with a red cross struck through it. I craned my neck to peer over the fence as I rode, even standing up on the foot pegs to be get a peek at what lay behind the fences. I even pulled over once or twice, to try and get a view of whatever the Bulgarian government was adamant that Johnny foreigner, this interloper from the west, should absolutely not take photographic evidence of back to his puppet masters in Whitehall.

I expected to see rows of nuclear silos, lines of T34 battle tanks, formations of MiG fighters, but all I saw was endless corn fields and a handful of chubby cows noisily emptying their bowels in only the way that cattle can.

I started to hit traffic on the outskirts of Sofia, the nation's capital. I got my first view of the city from the foothills of the rounded Vitosha mountain range on the outskirts of the city. There has been human habitation on the site of Sofia since at least 7,000 BC, and, at different times it has been occupied by Romans, Celts, Huns, Visigoths, Avars and Slavs, but the city isn't known for the winding streets and ancient architecture that mark most European cities. It is unfortunately dominated by the utilitarian, grey concrete buildings of the communism of its more recent history.

There are survivors and highlights of its long history. I rode past some of them as I navigated the city streets, The Largo, The National Theatre and the breath-taking golden dome of the Neo-Byzantine Alexander Nevsky Cathedral. There were no signs prohibiting photography, but there were suspicious looking police walking around the cathedral, and with the bike's exhaust drawing so much attention I didn't want to stop to take a chance.

Unlike Budapest, there are no bridges crossing rivers in Sofia, so I managed to successfully escape the clutches of the city and the confusion of the Cyrillic signposts without incident.

I hit the central plateau around noon and found myself to be starving. I have never really been able to go more than three hours without eating and I had long since burnt off the heady nourishment of my single pot noodle. More of the barbed wire fences with no photo signs had sprung up. They stretched for an eternity, hundreds of miles on either side, but I had long since given up the hope of seeing a nuclear tipped Intercontinental Ballistic Missile fired in a blaze of flame to streak into the sky. On the other side of the fences stretched only meadow and pasture. Perhaps the Bulgarians had invented some innovative manner in which to conduct arable and dairy farming and desperately wanted to keep the secret out of the greedy clutches of western capitalism.

The entire country seemed to lack essential infrastructure. I didn't see hotels, or restaurants, shops, or petrol stations. They must have existed, probably in the larger towns, but compared to Europe, and even more so the United States, for the road user, there was nothing to see and even less to buy.

And so, it was quite a surprise when I passed the outskirts of Plovdiv, I was amazed to see a sign pointing to a large warehouse type building on the horizon. There was large sign in the nearby field with an arrow pointing towards the building. In my long travels, the constant drip feed of signs written in Cyrillic must have had an effect on the wiring of my brain. The word that the strange mix of letters spelt was just too close to Supermarket to not be, and so I decided to take the chance.

I pulled off the road and followed a tarmac strip up a hill until I found myself in a vast and largely empty car park. There were three Lada's all painted in a different shade of cardboard. I have never understood communism. I get the premise of a system of social organization in which all property is owned by the community, and where each person contributes and receives according to their ability and need. That's fine. Take it or leave it. But why such a hatred of primary colours?

There was also a ZiL in what I took to be the manager's parking spot. I thought it was covered in dust, but when I got closer, I could see that the paint was just a flat and dusty beige that seemed to actively suck the sheen from the air that surrounded it. In front of the cars, looming over the space, shimmering in the heat of the day, was a building the size of a modern convention centre.

I parked the bike in one of the one-thousand empty parking spaces and walked in the hot sun towards the building. In the windows were orange placards with words written in Cyrillic and below that a price, obviously advertisements for the plethora of worldly goods that they sold. Slightly nervously, I licked my lips, rubbed a hand over my grumbling stomach and entered the store hoping to procure some bread and perhaps a humble tin of meat or fish.

The inside of the store was, by quite a margin, the most modern thing I had seen since leaving Austria. It was exactly like an American wholesale store, a Costco or a Walmart. Bright lighting, electric automated doors, blasting air conditioning and racks and racks, stacked to the ceilings. The only difference that I could see, which was admittedly a fairly substantial drawback for me, and judging by the car park, everybody else in Bulgaria, was that it only sold tractor tires. A vast and comprehensive range I have to admit. Huge, deeply treaded ones, ten feet in diameter, the sort you might find on a big green John Deere in the mid-west and skinny, smaller tires you might see on a smallholder's tractor from the 1950's, and everything in between. Many of the racks were completely empty, but where any rack stocked a product, it was a tractor tire.

I walked the length and breadth of the store, hoping and wishing for a single chiller cabinet that contained a single Bulgarian loaf, or just one of the hundreds of racks devoted to stocking five or six tins of potted meat. Nothing.

Back outside I stood for a while with a puzzled expression on my face. I couldn't quite rationalize what had just happened. Either this was a store that only sold tractor tires, as, admittedly, the evidence would suggest, or it was indeed a supermarket that had run short of everything most people needed and somehow over ordered a commodity not usually seen in a supermarket at all. But even if the store was in fact a TRACTOR TIRES—R—US, why one so huge? There were no tractors in the parking lot and as far as I had seen none in the fields surrounding us either.

During the morning's ride the sun had burnt off the small amount of cloud and the temperature had soared. I had only brought my thick leather gauntlets for the journey, and I was overheating badly. Before I got back on the bike, I took the decision to not put the gloves back on. Instead, I stored them under the tent, held securely by one of the bungee cords.

I immediately felt better. The gauntlets themselves were hot but the worst part was that they covered the cuffs of my battered old leather jacket. With the gloves off, a breeze was directed over my hands and up the sleeves of my jacket. The relief was immense and immediate, and I cracked the throttle to get to Turkey, and a source of food, as quickly as I could.

Shared Cucumbers

I said goodbye to Bulgaria and hello to Turkey close to the town of Edirne and immediately, finally out from behind the veil of the Iron Curtain, I saw a sign for a gas station, a restaurant and further up the road the sign for '*Ömür Camping Edirne*.' The heady comfort of capitalism. Decadence gone mad.

The campsite was great. It was such a sweet relief to be back in what felt like the west even though I was further east than I had ever been in my young life. There was a neat little toilet block with flushing toilets and hot showers and the site had a bonus lying in wait for me—a little restaurant that served hot food and cold beer.

I pitched the tent. The site was mostly empty, so I had my choice of pitches. As usual I chose the low lying one infested with biting ants, and immediately got my little wash bag and towel and walked across to take a shower. I hadn't had a proper wash since the deluge in Austria and I had to admit that the humming sound of my t-shirt kept me company on my short walk. The toilet block was basic, breeze block type construction, but it was spotlessly clean, so I hung my towel and stepped, soap in hand, into one of the stalls.

I turned the stainless-steel tap to get the water running and received an electric shock. It didn't throw me backwards or stop my heart, but it certainly made me pull my hand back and mutter "fuck," to myself. I tried again, tentatively tapped the tap, this time with my knuckles. Nothing this time, so I shrugged and turned that tap as far as it would go. The water got slowly hotter and hotter, and I held my head under the gorgeous torrent until I could stand it no longer. Covered in soap I reached for the tap to turn the heat down and, this time, I got a really good jolt that made me recoil and swear out loud again, "fuck, fuck, fuck," I seemed to remember saying, which was an amount of profanity directly proportionate to the amount of current that had coursed through my arm.

With the water still too hot and me still too sudsy I tried again—this time no shock. I assumed it was some kind of static build up so turned the hot water down, washed my t-shirt and finished my shower. I towelled dry and, squeaky clean, I stepped outside.

Seated on the wall opposite were three young men. They were all Turkish looking, dark hair and moustached with almond eyes. They all wore matching green Ömür Camping Edirne t-shirts and looked like they were on a break, chatting and laughing amongst themselves in the sunshine.

I walked over, to warn them about the electrocuting shower, but when I reached them, I foolishly realized I was only clothed in a towel and didn't speak more than three or four words of Turkish and not one of them related to showers or electricity. Still, now standing in front of them, mostly naked in my baby blue towel, I felt I had committed myself to some sort of action. I pointed at the shower block and mimed reaching out to an imaginary tap and then being electrocuted.

"Zap! Ow," I said hopping from foot to foot. I tried this several times, but they just nodded politely and smiled back at me. Finally, the man on the right stood to shake my hand.

"You biker? Yes? Suzuki? We like it very much. Come, my friend, come sit with us."

I gave up on my shower protest and sat down on the low wall and my new friend reached behind him to retrieve a cheap striped plastic bag filled with huge cucumbers. He passed me the largest one, and one to each of his friends, keeping the last for himself.

I wasn't certain what sort of friends I had made but I was intrigued as to how this new development might play out. I was sat in the sunshine holding my cucumber like some enormous green phallus wondering what would happen next when they all just started eating them like I have never seen a cucumber eaten before. Big bites, no salt, no dips, just big chunks of raw cucumber. They scoffed them like giant ice creams. My friend at the end looked across at me.

"Eat. Eat. Is good."

I have never relished a cucumber, but with the man's generously proportioned gift in my hand (yes, I just wrote that) I decided the best course of action was to simply join in. So, there we were, the four of us. Four young men, three swarthy, and one pale and sat only in a skimpy towel, munching away on long rude shaped vegetables. I wasn't entirely certain what this was, or what was happening, or indeed what might happen next, but compared to communism it was hedonism personified.

My Turkish friends, gardeners it turned out, had to go back to work, so I walked back to my tent with the whiff of another man's cucumber on my breath. I put on some fresh clothes and walked across to the little café, more than ready for a cold beer and some small animals roasted on a skewer.

The café was down a few steps, set into the ground, like a little sunken garden. Inside was a broad square with nine or ten trestle tables under a pagoda to screen the sun. I was seated only a minute when a pretty server brought me a menu and took my order for a beer.

When she returned, I ordered the '*şiş kebap*' I was enjoying getting back to an Arabic alphabet, I almost knew what I was going to get. While I waited for my food, the sun set and the lights around the pagoda came into sparkling life. It was serene and I was enjoying it very much. I ordered more beer and then my Shish Kebab arrived. Juicy, greasy, pungent chunks of lamb marinated in cumin and lime and skewered and grilled. I was just starting to devour the feast when a rumble of thunder was heard, and the heavens opened. Rain began to sweep across the campsite. By now there were a few other diners and while the pagoda provided some shade it did nothing to protect us from the rain.

I expected there to be a mass exodus, but nobody moved. I looked around me thinking to take the kebab back to my tent, but everybody carried on as though we were enjoying a picnic on a pleasant afternoon by the

Thames, so I too stayed and continued with my meal. As we ate, waiters came and went, took orders, and brought food while the downpour swept cutlery from tables and turned napkins into soggy piles of mushy pulp. Nobody looked up or considered leaving. Nobody remarked. It was most bizarre.

Then it got really strange. Because we were in a little sunken garden, and in a natural drain for the rest of the campsite, the seating area of the restaurant began to quickly fill with gurgling water. Inch by inch it rose. Water poured in. The water first lapped around the soles of our shoes, but it kept filling. I looked around me and saw people casually taking off shoes and rolling up trousers while continuing to chat and enjoy their meals. I took off my motorcycle boots and rolled up my jeans.

By the time I finished my kebab, I had my feet on the bench with my knees around my ears watching the waiters wade causally through a good foot and a half of standing water, balancing trays of drinks and dishes, the reflections of the lights dancing in the ripples of the wakes they left behind. It felt like a scene from the sinking of the Titanic where the band just casually ignore their impending doom and strike up a jaunty rendition of The Marriage of Figaro.

With dinner done, I dabbed the grease from my chin with a soggy napkin and waded bare foot, with boots held high and jeans rolled, through the now almost knee-deep water to climb the steps out of the submerged café.

As I headed back to my little tent I reflected on the trip so far, and this day in particular. The austerity and strictly regimented experiences of communist Hungary and Bulgaria, and the hidden tensions at play in Yugoslavia contrasted hugely with the laid back and plain insanity of Turkey. I was only a few hours in, but I was pretty sure I was going to enjoy it here. I fell asleep with a smile on my face dreaming of seeing Istanbul for the first time in the morning.

A Helping Hand

I naively thought that my approach to Istanbul would be framed by the glittering stretch of the Black Sea on one side, and the six towering pencil shaped minarets of the Blue Mosque on the other, all set against the elegant span of the suspension bridge that spans the Bosporus. The bridge stretches like the finger of God, from the bosom of Christianity to the west to be the first tender touch within the east, the land of its own cradle.

Of course, what really greeted me was an endless urban sprawl and it took me only seconds to become irrevocably lost in the maze of ancient side streets.

Everywhere I looked there was the bustle of the moment, the brittle friction of the intersection between east and west. European furniture outlets and car dealerships rubbed shoulders with street vendors and Tabac shops. Old men dressed in Fezzes playing checkers and smoking Hookah pipes, frozen in time, while business folks in suits from Milan and Paris hurried past to make the most of their lunch hour.

Carts piled high with cherries and dates, row upon row of mopeds and scooters, vans parked at jaunty angles while delivery men emptied their wares onto the dusty cobbles. The heat and noise and scents of the streets rose to assail my every sense. People teemed, tabbied cats slinked and dogs, not a pedigree amongst them, barked at everybody and everything. All around me was motion and commotion, the smell of the sewers mingled with the tang of the spices from the bazaar, sumac, cardamon, cumin, saffron and turmeric. At every junction sat a mosque, on every skyline a minaret and from every minaret a Muezzin's voice boomed, melodious and distorted by loudspeakers, the Adhan, the Muslim call to prayer.

I pulled over, overwhelmed by the frenzy and intense heat of the midday city, to consult my map. Still sat astride the bike I unfolded the map and laid it across the tank of the Suzuki. Heat rose like a furnace from the engine. I took off my helmet and retrieved a bottle of tepid water from the tank bag and took an unrefreshing gulp. The map showed the spread of Istanbul, vast and indecipherable, an Ottoman pirate map with its treasure obscured and hidden amongst its hieroglyphs.

When I set off that morning, from the campsite, I hadn't thought to work out where it was that I wanted to stay. I planned on being here for three or four nights and had lazily assumed I would simply ride into the city centre, stumble upon the touristy part of the city and easily find a hotel close to all the sights. Now immersed in the city, desperately drowning in its depths and complexity, that idea seemed beyond ludicrous.

My attention was suddenly seized from the map when I was astounded to feel the weight of somebody climbing to sit on the passenger seat of the bike behind me. I turned around, angry, ready to threaten, only to find a Turkish boy, perhaps fifteen sat there smiling back at me. He had a row of white teeth, a shock of jet-black hair that stood to attention on the top of his perfectly round head and eyes bright, the colour of shining onyx marbles.

"You lost boss? I take you where you wanna go."

For a moment I was rendered mute by confusion. There are times, moments and encounters, where the sum of life's experiences and teachings leave you lacking. This was one of them. I thought of telling him to just go to hell and get off my bike; but then what? I still had no idea of where I was, or indeed in which direction I was now facing.

I had long since lost any notion of north or south, east, or west.

"OK. I need a hotel. Not too expensive but something nice. Not a shithole you know?"

"I know one boss. Very good. Very cheap. I tell you where to go."

I still wasn't certain this was a good idea. I was lost in a city where I had only just taken my first breath. All was new and bitter with the taste of the unfamiliar. I was at sea here, had marked myself out to be the vulnerable foreigner, entirely alone. This kid could be anybody, a mule for a gang of sex traffickers, although what use the sex trade could have for my pale, pimply, unwashed body I wasn't certain. Perhaps they had seen the pictures of me with the Turkish camp boys and the cucumbers?

With a sigh of resignation and a shake of my head I pulled my helmet back on, and with the visor up, so I could hear the shouted instructions of my new friend, I cogged the bike into first gear.

"This way boss," I heard and saw a brown arm pointing forward.

The boy directed me left and right through narrow winding streets, underneath arches, through crowds of onlookers who turned to see the European riding his horrendously noisy bike, with one of their own street urchins perched on the back, shouting, and pointing.

I had no idea where we were heading and thought several times of stopping and ordering him off the bike, but something told me to keep going, to trust in the moment. I had crossed the Rubicon, carried my wobbly coracle down the steep riverbank and pushed off into the fast-moving stream.

We arrived at a busy intersection and my guide directed me to turn right onto a busy three lane carriageway. The road was clearly marked with white lines separating the lanes, but nobody seemed to care. Cars, scooters, and trucks simultaneously vied for every inch of the road, sometimes four or five abreast they swerved, gunned engines, blew black smoke from unsilenced exhausts, and continuously blared horns. I swallowed my unease and turned into the melee. No game of dodgems has been so frenetic. The big Suzuki was a liability in the heavy traffic. Small scooters blasted past me on both sides, huge trucks grazed my elbows. Buses, overloaded with every mix of humanity and a few random chickens pulled out into the stream of traffic without a backward glance or a hint of indication. I was forced to constantly swerve and veer away from traffic that just claimed the space I was currently not enjoying. The heat and noise of the city overwhelmed senses. My eyes stung from the combination of sweat and frantic concentration.

After about a mile of this ongoing madness, my passenger pointed across the road to our left.

"There, boss. Otel Kilim, you see it. Very good. Very cheap. Turn here," he shouted to make himself heard over the fray.

I looked but there was nowhere to turn. All the way along the centre of the road, separating the fast-moving lanes of traffic was a high concrete curb.

"Turn here. Turn here."

I didn't know what else to do so I slowed the bike causing speeding cars and smoking trucks to scream past us, horns honking and beeping. I swerved across the road and mounted the curb with a bump that made me rise up out of my seat. We bumped back down the other side and wove in and out of the fast-moving traffic like a frantic game of Frogger to reach the other side of the carriageway, panting and breathless.

I bumped over another curb to cross the pavement and parked the bike underneath a fire escape outside the hotel. My new friend jumped down.

"Otel Kilim!" he said, "Very Good. Very Cheap."

"Thanks mate," I said. It occurred to me that he would want some cash in exchange for his unlooked-for help.

I reached into my pocket and pulled out some Turkish Dinar notes and offered them to him, but he just smiled his bright smile, and shook his mop of hair.

"I show you the city now?"

"Err. I don't think so mate."

"Yes. Yes. Go drop off your bags. Meet me out here in ten minutes. I take you to a club I know."

"No. Thanks but I have to meet somebody," I lied, not very creatively. It was clear I was alone and a stranger, without friends in this city.

He didn't seem to care. My friend smiled back his beaming smile.

"OK boss," and with that he turned and walked away.

I stood for a moment in the heat of the city, wondering if I should call out to him and take up his offer of a tour of the city. But in the end, I admitted to myself that although I plainly was an innocent abroad, I was not a complete fucking idiot. I think it probably would have been OK, but who knows? I was entirely alone in this gigantic and puzzling city. Perhaps if I had gone with him, I would have been arrested later at some distant land border, found with a crazed expression, dilated pupils and two pounds of heroin stuffed up my arse.

I still had no idea where I was in the city, but I did know that I was outside a modern hotel. I could feel the welcoming blast of air-conditioning from the foyer doors pulling me like a dream walker into its chilly embrace.

I walked into the foyer just as another call to prayer boomed out across the city. I asked for a room, the receptionist spoke some English thankfully, and I hauled all my gear, in a couple of sweaty journeys up to a bright bedroom on the tenth floor that looked out over a skyline crowded with more minarets. I made one final trip to chain the bike to the iron fire escape, turned the bars to engage the steering lock and, hoping and muttering a silent call to prayer of my own that the bike would be safe, climbed the stairs back to my little room.

It was clean and sunny with a comfy bed and well provisioned with a sparkling En-suite and all had at only a few Dinars a night. I nodded in satisfaction.

"Very good. Very cheap," I said to myself.

The Muezzin

I stripped off my rancid riding gear and gave socks and skiddies a quick soapy rinse in the sink. I put on some shorts for the first time on this trip and had a walk to get my bearings and see the sights. The streets were an assault on the senses. They teemed with daily life, the minutiae of sixteen million souls all packed tightly together in this vibrant city, all telling their separate stories in the friends they made and the words they shared, bread broken in joy, while praise to Allah was uttered, almost without cessation, to the heavens.

Garments hung like prayer flags, drying from lines pitched from windows. Forbidding alleyways led between the old buildings, steps worn deep by the tread of millennia led to destinations and adventures that lay beyond imagination. I was finally in Istanbul, a place I had dreamed of visiting for months.

Originally called Byzantium and then Constantinople. Constantine named it after himself 330 years before Christ is fabled to have walked the earth, but there had been a city here since the Greeks founded it 1000 years earlier. Home at times of the Byzantines and the Ottomans, once it played a key advancement in the expansion of Christianity. Now it is a stronghold of Islam. The gateway to Asia. A city that reaches across two continents.

As I walked the streets, my eyes busy, the smell of acrid black coffee snared my attention and drew me to sit at a small wrought iron table painted a pink as bright as a peony, perched on the edge of the pavement outside a small and cramped cafe. Inside, locals sat wreathed in black fragrant smoke playing backgammon. The waiter, who took my order was surly and initially mistook me to be, and addressed me as, a German. I explained that I was English, and his demeanour changed to one of instant smiling friendliness.

It was a pattern that was repeated often during my stay. I wouldn't call it hatred, but this seeming wariness of the Germans was something I didn't really comprehend. Unlike nearby Greece, which was subjugated by Nazi occupation, Turkey signed a Treaty of Friendship with Germany at the beginning of the war and was never invaded or subjected to the famine and brutality that much of the rest of Europe endured. Turkey did finally declare war with Germany, but rather cleverly waited until 1945 to do so.

I ordered a Turkish coffee and had my small porcelain cup filled from a brass cezve, a small, long-handled pot in which the Arabica grounds had been boiled. I added sugar to the coffee and ate the Turkish delight that came with it. The blisteringly strong coffee and astoundingly sweet delight, flavoured with rosewater and cardamom snapped me wide awake.

I wandered the streets for a while, sweating in the baking heat of the day. Southern Europe was experiencing a heatwave, and all the news, on all of the TVs in the shop windows I passed, was filled with warnings of heatstroke and potential fatalities.

At any moment I expected to happen upon something famous and noteworthy, the Grand Bazaar or The Hagia Sophia perhaps. I craned my neck around street corners for a glimpse of the glistening blue of the Bosporus and stood on tip toe to peer over high walls hoping to catch sight of the Blue Mosque, but the busy, narrow streets went on without end. That was the problem in days before iPhones. You needed paper maps, and my Michelin Road map, the one I had brought with me, used a scale too large and useless to navigate city streets.

I popped into a little corner Tabac shop. It was cool inside, so I browsed the packed shelves for a few minutes, letting the sweat evaporate from my brow and holding out the fabric of my t-shirt from my clammy body. The shop sold everything. In addition to the usual tobacco, cigarettes, hookah pipes and clay pipes, the owner had filled the shelves with canned meats, bread, cakes, fragrant sacks of coffee, irons, cutlery, kettles, knives, hammers and nails, garden taps, hoes and four candles.

Behind the counter, row upon row of tall jars, made of blue-grey glass, contained sweets and candies of every hue. Newspapers and brightly coloured magazines filled every gap. The store's aroma was rich in tobacco and coffee, redolent of antiquity and history.

The old chap behind the counter watched me browse for a while.

"Deutsche?" he asked finally and with a note of suspicion in his voice.

"No. English."

"Aah. Welcome," he said with a broad smile and a clap of his weathered hands. "Welcome to my shop. What can I help you with?"

It was astounding how many people spoke really good English. I was endlessly grateful and at the same time, embarrassed that the most I could run to were a few sentences in French and the ability to swear and ask for beer in three or four others.

"I need a map of your beautiful city."

He ushered me to the counter and bade me sit on a wobbly wooden stool, so old it may have been one that Constantine himself had owned, while he strode around his shop looking for the maps. He was short and round with a kindly sun-darkened face and mischievous eyes, as dark as the coffee I had just consumed. We chatted as he walked around. He asked me where I was from and how I had got here, which airport I had flown into. When I told him I had ridden a motorcycle from England he reacted like I was Marco Polo or Vasco De Gama.

"No! Too far, much too far."

He returned with a yellowed and faded map, it might have been the first thing he placed in the window when he first opened his shop, he brushed a small, desiccated spider from it and handed me the map.

"Wait there my friend."

He disappeared into the back of his shop for a minute and returned with two water-beaded, ice cold cans of Coca-Cola which he set down next to the map.

"For you. Please, drink."

I picked up the coke and popped the tab and took a long drink, "teşekkürler," I thanked him in his native language. I am certain I mangled the word, but it pleased him enormously.

"You are a Turkish man!" he took a pause to laugh at his own joke, which I gladly joined in with, "now, what can I help you find?"

I spread the map on his crowded counter, "where am I?" I replied.

He looked at me with eyes wide and mouth agape and then his eyes twinkled, and he clapped his hands with a laugh. He laughed for quite a while, the sound of friendly hilarity at a foreigner's predicament in the city he knew and understood in a way that would forever be unreachable to me. His laughter was infectious, and I joined in. I suppose it was rather odd to have someone walk into your shop and ask where they were. Like those cheesy time travelling movies where the arriving adventurer always earnestly snatches a newspaper from a bystander to establish if it's the right time and place to stop Kennedy from being assassinated.

Finally, his laughter subsided, and he drew a finger along some of his familiar streets, finally stopping, his tobacco-stained fingernail to hover over a small cluster of buildings labelled the Feriköy Çağrı Market.

"You are here my friend."

I was quite a way from anything you would consider a tourist destination. Several miles away from the Bosporus and all of the sights I wanted to visit. We shook hands, I paid him for the map and offered to pay for the coke, but he waved me away with feigning offense. He told me to visit him again if I had the time before I left.

Back at the hotel I showered and asked at reception where was good to eat. To my delight, I was sent to the rooftop terrace where rows of tables were spread, covered with red check tablecloths, all arranged under threads of twinkling lights. The city was spread out before me. A messy sprawl of ancient tiled rooftops, of the homes and businesses. TV aerials, telephone cables, and power lines were as tangled as a ball of wool attacked by a kitten. Every washing line was decorated with undies and towels, shirts and skirts, splashes of colour against the austere back drop of the buildings. All so ugly it was breathtakingly beautiful.

The sun was slipping behind the minaret opposite the hotel. The minaret rose like a Saturn rocket, glowing blood red in the fading light, the end of the day ushering in the *Maghrib*, the first call to prayer of the new day, the

Islam day being counted as beginning at the setting of the sun. I was so close I could see the black cotton *thawb* clad Muezzin climb out onto the stone balcony at the top of the minaret and approach the microphone, could see the speakers arrayed to reach the residents. He began his chant, a voice strong and clear. It sang out across the skyline, not to be denied, a five-a-day demand that could always be heard, indoors and out.

I was, as usual, reminded of what a foreigner I was here. Entirely ignorant of the meaning of the words that he used to usher the faithful to their knees to face *qibla*, the direction of the Kaaba, the sacred Mosque in Mecca. I was ignorant; but the poignancy of the sound, in that time and place, although separated by my atheism, I was still deeply stirred by the emotions it evoked, sat as I was under a starless sky dominated by a rising sickle moon.

I was smiling, sunburnt, hot, and tired, captured by the mystery and endless drama of the city. I wiped the sweat from my brow, drained the remains of my sixth Efes beer and pushed another fork, loaded with grilled lamb and crispy, salty French fries into the ever-hungry hole in my face.

How Bazaar

I was awoken by the *Fajr,* the pre-dawn call to prayers. As it was the middle of July and the Fajr needed to be signalled before the first kiss of the sun's rays could touch the minaret, this meant the time was, not quite, six in the bloody morning.

I showered and got a breakfast on the rooftop, a simple meal of unleavened bread, a pungent Ezine cheese soaked in brine, and black olives. Back in the room I opened the windows and looked out at the day. The minaret had, thankfully, fallen silent. I leant out to look down onto the city street in time to see a gang of kids climbing like monkeys all over my bike. One impudent urchin was sat in the seat, leaning as far forward as he could, twisting the throttle. I couldn't hear over the noise of the city, but I swear he was making "*bruuuuuuum*," noises.

"Oi! Get off you little bastards," I shouted, "clear off."

They looked around, startled, wondering where the angry foreign shouting was coming from and then, with no sign of immediate retribution coming, continued in their play. I took the elevator down to the lobby and ran into the street waving my arms and shouting. The kids evaporated into the crowd like mist on a summer's day. I checked the bike and was relieved to see that although they had climbed all over it, they must have been incredibly careful and respectful. I turned the ignition key to find that the bike was in third gear and the lights and indicators were all on, but otherwise there wasn't a scratch, or anything broken. I took the key back to the room and leant out to close the window only to see that, like seagulls outside a beachside chip shop, they had flocked back and were now all seated in a single row of smiling faces on the seat.

I caught the rattling bus to the Grand Bazaar. The bus was packed, standing room only. I was jammed, sweating already, between a man dressed like a merchant banker, and an old lady, so small and wrinkled she could have been the unlikely result of a coupling between Yoda and E.T.

The passengers were the typically Turkish mix of western and eastern, smart gaudy city clothes, handsome faces, jarring against the contrast of discrete black hijabs, burqas and the occasional all concealing niqab. The bus bounced and jostled us over every manhole and pothole, and we all bumped around inside like a single conjoined entity. The bus seemed to stop every ten feet or so let five people off and ten people on.

By the time we got inside the walled part of the city I was pinned, arms tight against my sides, relying on the density and extreme proximity of the other passengers to keep me upright against the jolting, rolling motion of the bus.

Finally, I saw a sign for 'Kapalıçarşı', the covered market or Grand Bazaar, and elbowed my way as quickly as I was able, to reach an exit and step down from the bus. As I stepped from the shelter of the bus I was instantly consumed by the ferocious spice scented heat of the day.

Inside the Bazaar it was ten degrees cooler and, like everything in this place, ten degrees more mystifying. The Grand Bazaar is vast in a way that is hard to evoke but, given you have shelled out some of your hard-earned cash to read this I will make the attempt. I have lived in towns smaller than the Grand Bazaar. There are 4,000 shops in the market spread across a maze of sixty-one covered streets. The market is spread across an area of over 100,000 ornately carved and carefully architected square feet. The market is accessed through one of four wonderfully and evocatively named gates:

The *Sahaflar Kapısı*—'The Second-hand Book Sellers' Gate.'

The *Takkeciler Kapısı*—'The Skullcap Sellers' Gate.'

The *Kuyumcular Kapısı*—'The Jewellers' Gate.'

The *Zenneciler Kapısı*—'The Women's Clothiers' Gate.'

In times more ancient the market was organized by the type of goods sold, hence the names, but the market today has diversified beyond the ability to categorize. Furniture sellers rub literal shoulders with jewellery merchants, clock makers with handbag and clothing stores, carpets next to leather goods, perfumes with kebabs.

Exhausted by the wealth of goods, the noise, the constant movement and jostling of the crowd, I walked through the book sellers' gate back into the heat of the streets. I traipsed slowly north through the narrow alleyways, claustrophobically flanked on either side by three story stone buildings that felt like they were leaning in to impede progress.

I walked to the *Mısır Çarşısı*, the old Ottoman era spice bazaar close to the Bosporus. You don't need a map to find the spice market, just take a deep breath in through your nose and let your legs flap around in front of you until you arrive.

As soon as you enter, the bouquets and colours overwhelm the senses. The open sacks of spice tingle your nose and baffle the eyes. The taste of the spice is on the air and so the tongue. The merchants shout in competition, holding out handfuls of crimson Sumac berries, smoky Pul Biber, and eye-popping Pomegranate sour. The scents of the charcoal black Çörek otu and burnt ochre Saffron mingle with the perfume of the piles of yellow rosebud, jasmine, and fruit teas. There are Turkish delights in every colour and flavour; herbal remedies, dried apricots, figs, dates, strawberries, and kiwis; honeys and nuts of every variety, olive oil soaps and heady black Turkish coffee. A cornucopia, a bounty, an affluence, an exuberance, a luxuriance, a bountifulness of tastes, shades and fragrances, a truly thesaurus emptying experience. The whole experience was akin to being assaulted with a kaleidoscope in a Yankee Candle outlet.

I checked my watch and realized I had wandered for too long. I had booked a boat trip for my last adventure of the day. A ride along the mighty Bosporus itself. A boat trip is something I have always liked to do in a new city. It provides a different perspective. A city from the river, or ocean, looks fresh; it's like taking a good step back from a great painting, to lose the coarse brush marks of a Caravaggio, the harsh texture of reality, and blur the lines into something that instantly becomes more romantic and aesthetically uniform.

I caught the boat from a dock that lay in the shade darkened lee of the Atatürk Bridge that spans the stretch of water they call the Golden Horn, the major inlet of the Bosporus that defines the northern edge of 'old Istanbul,' the tip of which is the promontory of Sarayburnu. Such evocative names and rich sounds. Such history everywhere, it positively drips from the tongue.

The boat trip was an organized tour with commentary, and I enjoyed every moment of it. For one thing it was far cooler out on the water. For another, for the entire forty-five minutes of the trip the constant responsibility of being sole navigator and chief decision maker was taken from me. I sat in the prow of the boat, the sun turning the scalp through my thinning hair a startling shade of vermilion, and let the boat take me where it would while I listened to the tour guide.

We coasted past the Blue Mosque, officially the Sultan Ahmed Mosque. The Blue Mosque was built in the 17th century which pales in time when compared to its neighbour the far statelier Hagia Sophia, or '*Holy Wisdom.*' The Hagia Sophia was built in the year 532 by the eastern Roman Emperor Justinian I. Originally built as the Christian cathedral of Constantinople it became a mosque when the Ottoman empire finally conquered the city.

Our tour guide told us about how the property that lay along the shores of the Bosporus was amongst some of the most expensive in the world. But what I found far more interesting was when he told us that the Russian Navy had a huge submarine base in Sevastopol in the Black Sea to the north of us, and they were forced to use this narrow strait of water to get their submarines stealthily deployed into the Mediterranean Sea and beyond.

The fact that a Russian nuclear submarine could be below the keel of the boat right at that moment intrigued me enormously, and I admit I spent much of the rest of the trip torn between peering into the murky waters below, hoping to see the shape of a conning tower appear like a dolphin's back from the depths, and scanning the surface for signs of a periscope cutting a wake into the calm blue surface.

Soon the trip was done, and I took the bus back to my little hotel. I took a cold shower and sat panting in the air conditioning for an hour. For dinner, I considered walking to find a nearby restaurant but in the end, I climbed to the roof and sat at the same table as the night before, cold beer in hand, waiting for the dying rays of the sun to illuminate the minaret and bring my singing Muezzin out onto the balcony to welcome the new muslim day into existence, as he sent the words of the *Maghrib*, booming and wailing across the roofs of this wonderful city.

Bridge to Asia

I was awoken once more by the call of the Fajr. I had to say that if I had the boy on the back of the bike again, as I had when I first entered Istanbul, I might have added that in addition to the hotel being very good and very cheap, I would have asked for it to also be very bloody far from a bloody minaret, rather than directly across the bloody street from one. It was all well and good, and romantic and what not, listening to it on a rooftop under the stars with a frosty pint glass of beer in hand, but at 5:30 every morning it was beginning to get right on my tits.

Today I planned to get back on the bike and have myself a little excursion. This would be my last full day in Istanbul. Tomorrow, I planned to begin the journey home. But first I wanted to ride across the bridge and into Asia.

On my way, I planned to visit my shopkeeper friend again. Letting my mind wander away from the sights and sounds of Istanbul and begin to contemplate several long days back on the bike, I had started thinking about the cracked exhaust and the deafening noise that would accompany me all the way home. I had a long way to go and needed to affect some kind of repair. Suddenly a memory came back to me. My shopkeeper friend stocked jubilee clips, or worm drive clips as they are called in the USA, and sheets of aluminium.

After shooing a flock of street urchins away from the bike, turning off lights and indicators and making sure it was in neutral, I started the bike, cogged it into gear and rode through the streets I had earlier walked. It was only a short trip and I soon pulled up outside the shop and parked the bike. Before I took off my helmet my shopkeeper was out of the shop, pumping my hand in greeting.

"You came back! Come in. Come in."

In the pleasant shade of his shop, sat once more on Constantine's wobbly stool, he supplied me with another Coca-Cola, and I told him what I needed. Minutes later, with the aid of some borrowed tin snips, we had a broad strip of aluminium trimmed and wrapped tightly around the cracked segment of exhaust, all securely held in place by two large and shiny Jubilee clips.

I started the bike, and the difference was amazing. It was still loud, don't get me wrong, but it was of a volume that wouldn't attract the attention of the local militia or send me to the asylum, Edvard Munch's scream-like, with hands clamped over my ears.

I asked him the way to the freeway that led towards the bridge, and he drew a complex series of instruction in the air with his hands which I immediately forgot. I thanked him and we shook hands again and I rode away without even knowing his name.

Moments of serendipity, paths that converge, intersections of greetings, shared joy, hilarity and unlooked for friendships. And then a sudden but inevitable divergence, a separation. But a sweet one. One without loss or mourning. Such are the happenstances that lie in wait for the traveller alone, some hard and painful for sure, but most beneficial for the heart and the soul, confirmation of the common decency of most people.

I picked up signs for the Atatürk Bridge, the same bridge close to where I had boarded the boat the day prior. I crossed the Golden Horn, the sun high in the sky sending blinding reflections, flashes of light to sparkle from the gently winding strait. The road took me east and then north, past churches, ancient monuments, crumbling city walls and domed mosques, with minarets soaring in their attempt to pierce the sky. The song and dance of Istanbul played out all around me. Bustle and noise, commerce, and conversation. The traffic was heavy everywhere but every now and again, between the buildings that crowded the road I was rewarded with the steely blue glint of the Bosporus.

I was following the road north which ran parallel to the sea. It took me past the Dolmabahçe Palace, the grand domed home of the Sultan, Abdülmecid I who commissioned it in 1843. It later became the home of the Ottoman government. Then the road veered left, away from the sea to sweep me onto the famous and enigmatic Bosporus Suspension Bridge and towards Asia.

Eight lanes wide and 3,500 feet in length the bridge is supported by two suspension towers that leap 541 feet above the Bosporus itself. The views from the centre of the bridge were spectacular. The tiered skyline of the city behind me, the crystal blue of the Bosporus on either side and the rising, barren, camel-coloured hills of Asia in front of me. In seconds I was magicked across, transported from one continent to another.

My destination wasn't far. In the hotel I had asked where in Asia you could get good views of the city, and everybody said the same thing—Çamlıca Hill. It was only a few miles inside Asia.

Back then, in 1986, what you got for no money at all was what was advertised—a hill. It was a good hill. 1000 feet above sea level it afforded splendid panoramic views south across the city, the Bosporus, and the mouth of the Golden Hind, but it was just a hill. If you visit nowadays there is a tower there, designed to look like some enormous tulip, which takes you an additional 1000 feet into the air. The tower has observation decks, restaurants, a library, an exhibition hall, and toilets. Thinking about toilets, I needed a pee myself, and given I was entirely alone on my dusty little hill I had a quick one behind a scrubby but increasingly damp bush.

Back at the hotel I checked through all of my equipment in preparation for leaving. I scrubbed some socks and t-shirts in the sink and added my washing to the skyline by hanging them out of the window like the native of the city I pretended to have become. I was quite sad to leave. I loved this city. Its constant noise and colour, the way the shades and tints of the buildings and its skyline morphed throughout the day as the sun tracked its slow way, east to west.

Istanbul is an enigma. Its identity was unclear to me. It was like two different coloured paints poured onto a blank canvas. The colours stood starkly apart in places but in others they had mixed and created new shades. Islam and

Christianity. Modern and ancient. The city's inhabitants' lives were ground together in a gigantic granite mortar that brimmed with the hot spices of Islam and the cold herbs of Christianity.

I was also going to miss sleeping in a comfy bed with a roof over me in air conditioning so cold that it puckered the skin, and a restaurant on the roof that served me warm lamb and frosty beers whenever I wanted it.

While I had acted the tourist, the heat index had continued to steadily increase. Over the next few days, the metrological office was forecasting a daily temperature of 40 degrees centigrade, 104 degrees Fahrenheit.

I called home from the hotel foyer, pushing dinar coins like a Las Vegas one armed bandit addict as quickly as I was able into the payphone slots, while the phone company sent a continuous series of loud beeps to let me know I was running out of credits. I spoke to my Mum to let her know I was still alive. Her voice was soft and distant over the crackle of the wire. I could barely tell it was her. She sounded small and old and suddenly I missed her.

I told her that I would be leaving Istanbul in the morning and planned on returning through mainland Greece and then back up the western coast of Yugoslavia. I told her I would see her in a just a few more days, and then the beeps outpaced my ability to feed the coins into the slots and we were cut off with a loud click.

I stood listening to dial tone for a few seconds. The one thing she had confirmed for me was that my brother Dave was in Yugoslavia. He had ridden his Moto Guzzi to Yugoslavia and should be somewhere on the Adriatic coast by the time I got there. We were hoping to meet up when I arrived, but given mobile phones hadn't been invented it seemed an unlikely logistical proposition. The Adriatic coast runs for well over 2,000 miles, so finding Dave would be unlikely, he would be the literal needle in the haystack.

I knew I should take the last opportunity and walk to find a different restaurant, explore more of what the city had to offer, to perhaps eat something other than a lamb kebab, but to be honest the call home and the sound of Mum's voice had made me feel lonely and homesick. Eating alone every night, watching others sat with friends, lovers, and children, all laughing and chatting together, sharing the experiences and tales of their day was taking its toll. For the first time in my young life, this trip was teaching me that loneliness is often strangely exacerbated by the proximity of others.

So, an hour later I was back, seated in my roof top hotel restaurant, eating lamb, and watching the sun dip below the horizon. As the sun set the city aflame, I pushed lumps of squishy cheese firmly into both ears just as my wailing Muezzin strode out onto his balcony.

As night scattered the stars like crap dice across the velvet sky, I discovered that even Turkish cheese in the ears was insufficient to block out the warble of the Maghrib. Another day had begun in Istanbul.

A Pirate's Draft

The hotel breakfast was just being set up so, while the staff were otherwise distracted, I snuck in and, feeling like a cat burglar stealing the sultan's jewels, put two bread rolls and a napkin containing salami and olives into my helmet. I was back! Helmet lunch was secured.

I left before first light. The night had brought a fleeting chill to the city streets. They were deserted, just me and the windblown, scattering litter of the prior day. I unlocked the bike and wheeled it to the curb. The Otel Kilim had been a good choice, and I would miss its air conditioned cool, its hot and cold running water and the comfy bed. I looked back one last time at the light that poured from its welcoming windows and then pulled in the clutch and fired the bike into life. Time to move on.

The city streets were dark. Not many streetlights existed to light my way back through the tangled maze of ancient side streets, and back to the highway I needed to find to whisk me away from the city sprawl. I saw the numbered sign for the road I needed and took the second exit onto the on ramp. It led me down a steep gradient towards the still quiet road out of town. I guess I was still waking up, confused by sleep because as I rolled the throttle back to match highway speed, the world lit up and two giant saucers of headlights were suddenly rushing towards me.

I had somehow, in my confusion, turned onto the off ramp and was now riding on the wrong side of the road, against oncoming traffic. The headlights belonged to an enormous cement mixer truck who was exiting the road. I swerved violently, and he blared his horn as he blasted past, only an inch or so from me and my bike. I managed to get the bike slowed enough to judder to a panicked stop on the rough and litter filled piece of land that ran beside the slip road.

"Christ on a fucking bike, what are you doing you utter knobhead," I muttered in a quiet reprimand to myself, in shocked disbelief at my almost fatal error.

Luckily, there was still almost no traffic, and the slip road was wide just enough for me to carefully, with my left foot on the ground, slip the clutch and to ride the bike in a tiny circle until I faced the correct direction. With a quick glance behind me, I quickly rode back up the off ramp, heart pounding, still chastising myself as I rode. I turned a very cautious left and got on the highway at the correct junction.

Now thoroughly wide awake, senses literally jangling, I made good progress through the deserted suburbs. By the time of Fajr, the first call to prayer began to ring around the streets, I was watching passenger airliners stacked, blinking navigational lights bright against the waking sky as I passed the International Airport southwest of the city.

I finally broke free of the urban clutter as I crossed a small bridge that spanned a muddy estuary. The houses and markets, churches and mosques slipped away, receded from me as I rode into the increasing heat of the day. Low rolling hills, lush and vital with still green corn and golden maize replaced the dusty streets, bringing much needed colour, a balm for the eyes after the harsh monochrome of the city. Every now and again I spotted a small farm sat, squat on the horizon, a brilliant splash of white against the azure backdrop of the endless sky.

Istanbul was like a vast singularity, reaching out into the countryside with its influence, snaring all manner of life in its relentless pull towards its centre. The further I rode the less I saw, all businesses and means of commerce had sought the city to survive, sucked into its circle of influence, leaving the countryside pretty but desolate. No cafes or houses, garages, or hotels.

I was more than thirty miles from the city before signs of small settlements and towns began once more to appear. I saw a sign on the outskirts of Silivri for a restaurant, the 'Bati Balik.' The map showed a small port town and intrigued, I turned off the main road to take a peek, and perhaps sit by the Mediterranean and eat my stolen lunch.

There was a port but the whole place was dismal. A 1970's sand coloured concrete tragedy littered in broken glass and graffiti. A handful of downtrodden miscreants dressed in the same sand grey as their surroundings shuffled about.

The town somehow managed to make even the Mediterranean it bordered look dull and scruffy. It reminded me very much of the Star Wars town of Mos Eisley, the spaceport on Tatooine that Luke Skywalker visits at the beginning of his journey, and the wisdom in the words and voice of Sir Alec Guinness as he described it.

"*You will never find a more wretched hive of scum and villainy. We must be cautious.*"

I decided to move on.

The road swept me inland, away from the coast. The bike thumped away in a reassuringly regular fashion, pulling the long miles beneath me. The sun rose high into the sky and beat down on bare hands that held the handlebars, turning them the colour of hazelnuts. My thighs burned beneath my denim jeans and the stream of air through the vents of my helmet was a blast furnace.

I pulled over to refuel the bike close to the little rural town of Aleybey. I bought a cold bottle of water from the little store and found a neat patch of grass underneath an ancient pine tree that grew at the back of the petrol station. I sat for a while in the pleasant shade to drink and slowly eat my stolen salami sandwich and to pop the salty black and green olives one by one into my parched mouth.

By the time I got to the border with Greece it was sweltering. I had to queue for quite a while at the Greek border. There didn't seem to be any reason for the delay, the Greek border guards were just taking their own sweet time. As I waited, the sun beat down and I could do nothing but sit in the glare of the blistering sunshine, sweating and panting. The ferocious unrelenting heat was slowly dehydrating me, and the first pang of a headache pierced my skull while I waited for the next car to be waved forward to the red and white striped barrier, to have his paperwork slowly scrutinized. I removed my helmet and sat astride the bike, engine off while I waited for my turn.

Each time a car was waved forward I was forced to balance the helmet back on my head, pull in the clutch, turn the ignition, and cog the bike into gear to trundle slowly forward ten feet and then find neutral and turn the hot bike off again.

At last, it was my turn to advance up to the barrier. I took off my helmet and handed the bored looking guard my passport. He flicked through it in a thoroughly disinterested manner. He walked across to the little hut that stood close by the barrier and stamped a blank page with the date and place of my entry.

He leant on the counterweighted end to raise the barrier and I was through, crossing the river Maritsa that carves out the border between the two countries.

I changed languages and currencies once more, this time Dinar to Drachma. It was a strange sensation travelling in the pre-European Union days. Even though, at least initially, the geography initially remained the same, when crossing between one country and another you always got the spine-tingling frisson thrill of *knowing* you were somewhere very different, both ethnically and culturally. It was something visceral, it *felt* different. The air somehow smelt more Greek, the architecture more Grecian, the cheese more Feta(y), and the roads a bloody disgrace.

And of course, with the language change, the road signs switched. I saw a road sign for Alexandroupoli—the letters were absolutely unrecognisable to me. I only knew it must be Alexandroupoli because it was the first large town shown on my map close enough to the border.

The bloody Greek alphabet. It was even worse than the Cyrillic, a navigational conundrum, entirely indecipherable, especially when on a moving motorcycle actively trying to correlate the western names on my paper map with the signposts.

The afternoon slowly wore on and the heat continued to intensify. There were plenty of hours left in the day, but it was torture on the bike, and the coast lay only an hour south of me. I thought a campsite by the Mediterranean might just be the tonic I needed.

I headed south to pick up the coast road and as soon as I did, I started to look for a campsite. This wasn't the most touristy area but still, pretty soon, I saw a sign for 'Municipal Camping.' It was a big site with pitches set between tall shady poplars and sand that ran down to the crystal blue and tempting sea. I saw two spotless, gleaming BMW motorcycles parked by the side of an expensive looking tent so knew there would be Dutch or German bikers nearby. I parked my dusty, battered looking Suzuki close to their pitch and put up the tent.

By the time I finished I was soaked with sweat. I took a bottle of water out of my tank bag and tried a glug, but it was so hot it burned my throat. I poured the overheated contents around the base of the nearest poplar and walked to the camp shop to get something cold out of the fridge. When I got there it was closed and my need for water was extreme.

By the toilet block I saw a tap. Above the tap was a sign, the picture of a skull and crossbones, painted black on white, presumably to warn the unwary of the contents not being entirely drinkable. But when I experimentally turned the tap the water flooded out, clean and cold onto the ground. I swilled my face and tasted the water. It was fine, sparkling and refreshing. Thinking that, even here in Greece, health and safety had gone mad, I filled my bottle, downed the contents, and refilled it. I walked slowly back to the tent and given it was still only mid-afternoon, I changed into some European budgie smugglers and took a towel down to the beach for a swim and a sunbathe.

Two hours later I woke up with a tingle of the skin and a gurgle of the guts. I blinked open my eyes to see my torso had been burned the colour of a carpaccio of beef by the ferocity of the afternoon sun. Simultaneously, the first of the crippling stomach cramps doubled me up, and the noise of a toddler letting air slowly out of a balloon, accompanied by the odour of death, informed me that I really needed to make an urgent trip to the toilet block. I was shivery and burning up at the same time. I couldn't tell if it was heatstroke or dysentery.

It was both.

Sickness

I had quite the rough night. As it turned out I had quite the rough few days to look forward to. Of course, I shouldn't have disregarded the sign and drunk the poisonous pirate water. I was an idiot. Perhaps if it had only been the diarrhoea, I would have been ok, but I was also badly sunburnt. Sore and sick I sat in my tent sweating buckets and shaking like a shitting dog, cramping, and groaning. Gastric distress doubled me into the foetal position, knees tucked in pain, making gurgling and whoopee cushion noises, interrupted only by the occasional, wide-eyed and buttock clenched sprint to the toilet block.

I had managed to make a couple of quick trips to the camp shop without soiling myself, although it was a close call on both occasions. Even the mild bump of each cautious step threatened to let something loose and hot, slip from liquid bowels. I bought some clean, cold bottled water and sat inside the tent, sipping it in the shade with shaking hands, where the temperature was only 103 degrees.

I lost an entire day in that manner, white knuckled, red-faced and brown trousered, and from more detail than that I will spare you. The next day I popped my head out of the tent to find the Dutch/German bikers camped next to me, comfortably seated on little folding stools making breakfast. They had a full four ring gas burner and pots and pans and even proper ceramic plates with knives and forks. The pans were filled with sausages and fluffy scrambled eggs. I shook my head in disbelief. This wasn't camping. What I was doing was camping. Taking risks and living life on the jagged edge.

They turned out to be Dutch and looked up in horror when I first unzipped the tent and stuck out my swollen, crimson, unshaven visage. I was terribly sunburnt. It must have looked like somebody had painted blue eyes onto a baboon's arse. Of course, they were really lovely, pretended not to notice my jaded appearance, and asked me to join them for breakfast. I politely declined for reasons of a digestive nature. I was still in such a delicate condition that sipping only still water had the same effect on my sphincter as eating a rancid lamb madras.

The Dutch lads and their girlfriends were heading to Istanbul and then onwards into Asia and they asked me to join them. I honestly think they had discussed my welfare when I had popped off on one of my frequent, but irregular, sprints to the toilet block, and had come to the agreement that an intervention on my behalf was needed, that I should not be left to my own devices. At any cost. But I had to say no. My future lay in the opposite direction. I had already lost a day and needed to be moving on.

The next morning, moving around the site on wobbly legs, I packed the tent and the bike. I felt sick and weak, hands shaking, still sweating from fever and disease. I was dreading the day. The forecast was for another temperature record-breaking day. The roads were bumpy and my guts unreliable, a terrible combination. I managed to painfully pull the helmet over my sunburnt, raw, and now peeling face, and with a wave to my worried looking Dutch neighbours I hit the road again.

I got lost near Kyklopas, took the wrong turn when I just couldn't make any sense of the road signs. I couldn't match the place name to anything, anywhere on my map and only realized I must have gone wrong when the road slowly wound upwards over a hill, and the tarmac turned to rutted dust where a straggly brown goat stood, horns lowered, blocking my path.

Back on the right path I pulled into a decrepit petrol station that lay in the deep shadow of the Pangaion mountain range. An old Greek chap, skin as tough, olive brown and wrinkled as a pachyderm, finally made his weary way out of the shop and with a friendly nod filled the bike with one hand, while drawing deeply on a black and smoking cheroot with the other. With each deep inhale the tip glowed a bright and dangerous red, held only inches from the stream of smoky blue gasoline.

On the road back out of town, on the far side, I stumbled across a small sandy beach and pulled over. I ate my lunch and drank some water and then, unusually for me, took a selfie. Of course, in those days taking a selfie involved a little more than flipping the camera on your phone and snapping away. I found a fence that was about the right height to frame me and the bike, balanced the camera carefully on the fence, checked all looked ok through the little viewfinder, set the cameras delay timer and ran back into shot. The cover photo for this very book is the picture that I took that day. Somewhat familiar eyes in a face I almost remember look back at me from depths of time that have slipped by and scattered. I look hot, dusty, and tired.

I had no idea where I was at the time, other than that I was somewhere in Greece. It was close to thirty years later, after I had written this account of my travels, that I posted the picture on social media, in a group for adventure motorcyclists, that I received a random comment from one of its members who informed that he lived in the little town in the background, and that it was called Kavala.

As I was packing the camera back in my tank bag, some German bikers saw me and pulled over. We chatted for a while in broken English. When they found out I was heading back through Yugoslavia they warned me.

"Be very careful. There are many police speed cameras there. The fines there are very large."

They were all dressed in matching Dainese leathers with expensive helmets, brand new BMW motorcycles with matching panniers. Everything sported an expensive logo. They all looked like they could afford a fine or ten to me, but I took their advice in the spirit it was meant, and we nodded our farewells.

Back on the bike I continued to ride west. Sometimes the Mediterranean tracked my slow progress, at other times I was whisked into the dusty hills, but always the sun beat down. On the outskirts of Amphipolis, I had to make a difficult decision. I had hoped to get inside the southern border of Yugoslavia by the end of the day, but I felt truly dreadful. I was still very weak and shaky. The heat was dehydrating me more than my sick body could take. My only other option was to try and find a campsite inside Greece and get some rest.

I unfolded my map to look at options. Just a little further west and south lay the peninsula of Halkidiki, stretching its three fingers out into the Mediterranean. I didn't want to ride too far south and have to re-trace miles again in the morning, but not far away was a small town called Stratoni, perched above a sandy beach. I was sure there would be a campsite close by, and it was less than an hour's ride away.

The road took me down a fast, winding coastal road, bottle green groves of twisted and gnarled, ancient olive trees on one side and the sparkling cyan sea on the other. The first finger of Halkidiki lay like a two-day bruise across the wide bay. I swept through the town of Olympiada, and then began to climb into the hills to cross the short span of land that separated me from my goal.

For once the roads were excellent, long curves tightened into hairpins, flashes of the sea, like gifts, were glimpsed through the heavy firs whose tops ran parallel with the road. The cliffs to the left of me dropped away increasingly precipitously and finally, towards the end of an arduous day, I remembered why I was here. Just to be young and free on a fast bike, riding hard and swiftly through a series of sweeping curves on such a wonderful day in a country never seen before. Bliss. Despite my fever and heaving guts I was in heaven again.

Finally, the road levelled and then began to descend back towards the sea and the small town of Stratoni hove into view below me. The houses were white adobe walls set beneath orange clay roofs, an untidy cluster of homes on a narrow flat plain stretched between the green wooded hills and the crescent of golden sand that broke the sea into milk bottle-coloured flecks.

At the bottom of the hill, I saw a sign for camping and less than ten minutes later I was busy sweating while I pitched my tent, listening to the pops and pings of a cooling engine. I parked up next to two BMW tourer motorcycles, all with branded luggage and fancy hard panniers. The noise of my rattling, backfiring arrival had drawn two stereotypes from their comfortable tent. They were blue-eyed, blond, and tall and called themselves either Jürgen and Günter or Hans and Klaus, I forget which. Unusually for bikers they looked down their Teutonic noses at the jaded and battered condition of both me and my bike. The oil from the leaking cylinder head sent smoking blue tendrils into the air, the Jubilee clips and jury-rigged repair to the exhaust, the yellow plastic bag and faded bungee cords that contained my worldly possessions. We exchanged minimal pleasantries, but they did warn me, echoed the warnings of the other German bikers that I should go easy in Yugoslavia, the speed traps were everywhere and the fines for being caught, outrageous.

My attention and patience were interrupted by the sight of, across the green lawn, a small, neat bar booming out Barry White songs. The smell of grilled meat reached across the campsite to snare my nostrils. It drew me instantly away from any further judgement from the German boys.

The lamb was pink and greasy, marinaded in mint and thyme and grilled to perfection, salty and delicious. The salad was chunks of tomato, the aroma of which rose earthy and spicy. The crumbled feta was tangy, rich, and peppery. I washed it all down with a couple of Mythos beers, dry and refreshing.

The light of the sun faded behind the mountains and the lights of the bar flickered into yellow life to bathe the bar and its few patrons in soft lights whose shadows lazily swung in the warm breeze from the sea. Barry White's deep rumbling rendition of 'You're the First, The Last, My Everything,' faded out to be replaced by the first bass notes of, 'I've Got so much to Give,' and I realized that, at that moment, so did I. The food and drink had been too premature for my delicate constitution, my stomach bulged and rumbled and, twenty seconds later the bill was paid, and I was waddling, eyes wide and knees clenched tightly together, as quickly as it was safe to do so, back towards the toilet block.

Broken Bottles

I had another rough and shaky night but, in the morning, I did feel a little better. I brewed some tea and while I waited for the water to boil, I looked again at my increasingly dog-eared map. The direct route to the Adriatic coast lay due west, but that way was denied to me, for that road lay through Albania, and Albania in the 1980s was an enigma. It was still a country of closed borders and secrets.

Albania and Yugoslavia had initially followed similar trajectories after the end of World War II. Both had joined the Soviet Union, and both had been run by a single dictator for many years. In Yugoslavia it had been Tito, and in Albania it had been Hoxha. Enver Hoxha seized power and implemented his own brand of communism, ruthlessly executing any, and all political rivals. Up to 25,000 people were killed during this tumultuous period.

The country split with the Soviet Union in 1956, but instead of beginning to embrace western ambitions, as Yugoslavia had done, Hoxha's aspirations and hopes lay to the east, towards China and Mao Zedong. Hoxha locked the country down, banned international travel and outlawed religions of all kinds.

There was one other way the two countries had paralleled each other. Five years ago, Tito had died, and earlier in the same year of my travel, 1986, Hoxha had also died.

Change was on the way, but it would be too late to help me. I would have to take the long way around, ride back into Yugoslavia and journey north, skirting all the way around Albania's lengthy borders, before heading back west, to pick up the Adriatic coast.

I packed up and headed back north, tracing the curve of the meandering Vardar River that emptied into the broad swampy delta of the Axios National Park to my west. The landscape swung between high arid hills and lush river valleys.

At the little town of Tsoliades, I said farewell to the Greek alphabet and crossed back, once more, into the Cyrillic and familiar embrace of Yugoslavia. In my ride south to Istanbul, the greatest bulk of my miles had been through Serbian territories. Here I found myself in Macedonian land, mountainous and rural. I was still riding in the valley of the Vardar but to my left the heavily forested flanks of the Jakupica Mountain Range rose like a dark menace to tower over the valley. The lofty, bald granite peak of Solunska Glava pierced the clouds that swirled above the tree line, where the impenetrability of the rocks finally forced the pines to relent in their ascent.

I passed the town of Gnjilane and was reminded of an incident that had occurred in the town only a few months before my arrival. I had read about it in the newspaper prior to setting off and the name of the town and the story had stuck with me for reasons of which will become clear.

Now, depending on your viewpoint, the incident I am about to recount was either tragic or darkly comedic. I always favoured the dark side of any story that ends up in a good old-fashioned hospitalization. Unfortunately, as much as this one had made me chuckle, the story had also been picked up and used by the media to create a point of heated contention between the Serbian and Albanian populations in the region. It had become known as the '*The Martinović Affair*,' and had been turned into a cause célèbre in Serbian politics. What should have been a local incident had been used to take another incautious step down the slippery road towards the increasingly divided and nationalistic nature of the country I was riding through.

One short version of the story is that our hero, a local Serbian farmer called Đorđe Martinović had balanced a beer bottle on the end of a stick in one of his fields and then intentionally inserted the bottle into his anus for the means of personal sexual gratification. I'm guessing it was a fairly quiet day. Whatever right? Each to his own. Not my thing, but I guess it all makes the world go around. I will grant him that it is very rural there and the number of cinemas, skating rinks, theatres and other non-anally based distractions are genuinely minimal.

That might have been the end of the story, but somewhat unfortunately, for Martinović at least, the bottle broke inside him and became wedged there. He had to be treated in hospital for some fairly serious injuries. During his hospital stay, a curious Doctor surely asked him how the offending bottle might have got where it did, and Martinović did what most of us would have done and, allegedly, lied. He told a story of two Albanian men who had confronted him in his field and, for no good reason other than the fact that he was Serbian, viciously assaulted him with the bottle.

Martinović's story sparked outrage and a *lot* of anti-Albanian sentiment. An investigation to establish the truth was set in motion. Now, depending on who was asking, Martinović's story began to swing wildly between an admission of doing the act to himself, and one of him being brutally assaulted. Even the Yugoslav secret police and military intelligence got involved, all the while, the anger and divisions would only increase in fervour and vim.

In the end, Martinović's story became so jumbled and obfuscated that the truth became impossible to establish. But the harm had been done, to the accord between Serbians and Albanian's living in the area, and presumably to Martinović's arse.

I rode into the Bjeshkët e Nemuna National Park in what is now modern Kosovo. Mountains rose from the deciduous and coniferous forests, large placid lakes, milky blue, stretched across clearings. The air and feel were almost Alpine, even the houses that perched precariously on tangled rocks above the road felt Tyrolean.

The roads were surprisingly good, well paved, and smooth, and I carved my way through them enjoying the day. It was cooler in the mountains and the air that rushed in through the neck of my leather jacket eased the itching of my slowly healing sunburn. In every direction the views were spectacular. Rugged hills, some wreathed in a high mist snaked into the distance for as far as the eye could see. The Suzuki was nimble and an easy ride around the endless sweeping bends. At times I was high in the mountains looking down into a verdant valley and the next minute I was surrounded by forestry.

Small, rural towns, like the ones I had encountered in Serbia, were dotted along the route. Just like Serbia, Macedonia had the feel of a country left behind by the twentieth century. Almost without fail, my arrival made the men and women, all dressed in traditional garb, stand still, and point at the strange, helmeted rider who rode his raucous machine through their quiet lives.

I was really flying, no traffic anywhere on the roads, making great progress when I came to the edge of a small town and saw, just too late, a car parked by the side of the road. Out of the window an arm held something black, pointing back down the road in my direction. Damn it. A speed trap. As I approached the car, still trying to casually drag the brake to slow down, he flashed his lights, and I pulled over to stop alongside him.

The cop motioned for me to remove my helmet and took a step back in fright at the first sight of my blistered, peeling, ruby red face. He checked my paperwork and babbled away in Serbian or Bosnian for a while, pointing to road signs that very clearly displayed the speed limit I had just broken by a very wide margin indeed. I nodded along amicably enough, dreading how much this was going to cost me. I wasn't certain how many Yugoslavian Dinars I even had left.

If I couldn't pay what would happen—would they hold me in prison somewhere? While I mentally panicked, the officer busily wrote me a ticket and handed it to me. I did a quick currency conversion and almost laughed in his face. The fine for breaking the speed limit by a good forty miles per hour was the equivalent of less than a fifty pence piece. Who knew Germans had a sense of humour. I almost popped a wheelie away from the cop—catch me if you can at those prices.

As the day wore on, I continued to make good progress, but I was beginning to feel tired again. The cool of the hills had helped, but this part of Yugoslavia was vast and the required diversion I needed to take around Albania's border was lengthy. It was already mid-afternoon, six hours of almost continuous riding when I crossed a bridge over the enormous, glassy expanse of Lake Skadar and then, through the trees, the coast appeared like a balm for tired eyes, a pleasing easement from the endless green of the forest.

I decided to stop at the very first town I came across. Fortunately, that town was Sveti Stefan. It is a russet roof topped huddle of homes that sits on a thin peninsula stretched out like a tear drop into the sparkling sea, surrounded by oyster pink sandy beaches. Astoundingly beautiful.

I had a walk around the town and then rode a mile back into the hills where I had seen a camping ground. I pitched the tent, had a good stretch, and walked across to the shower block; soap wrapped in the towel under my arm. Halfway there a small Trabant car pulled across the path in front of me and a woman's voice called out in Macedonian.

I approached the car, apologizing as I did so, "I'm sorry, I only speak English."

"Ah. Do you know the time please?"

I checked the time on my wristwatch and, rather than attempt to perform some complex translation, I leant into the car with my wrist tilted so she could read it for herself. As she read the time, I glanced into the car. There was a man, seated behind the steering wheel and the woman beside him. They were both in their late twenties, young and attractive. In the back seat were three children, all between five and eight. They were all looking at me, all smiling, white teeth in sun-tanned faces. And they were all absolutely naked. Not a stitch in sight, seated with bare buttocks on the hot vinyl seats. I tried not to stare at the naked lady for too long, but I have to admit things had got fairly awkward before I managed to tear my gaze away and continue my walk, with a slight shuffle and a towel held low, towards the showers.

I shook my head as I walked away thinking that maybe, it was I who had screwed up. It wouldn't be the first time after all. Perhaps, I reasoned, I had somehow inadvertently found my way onto a naturist only campsite and I was the odd one out here, dressed in my bashfully minded socks and shirt. But no. I looked about me, everybody else on the campsite was clothed and doing normal camping things, grilling hamburgers, playing ball, and reading magazines in uncomfortable chairs. All properly dressed in shorts and t-shirts.

Then I realized that the car had come in through the campsite gates. The naked family were returning from some sort of excursion, they must have been out all day with bums, boobs and other uglies dangling in the sea breeze. Bat shit crazy—just saying.

Hey Bro

I woke with a buzz of excitement, and it wasn't long before I had the tent down and the bike packed. I had a quick look around the camp in case any naked ladies were wandering around looking to establish the time of day, I had my watch ready, but there were none to be seen. Shame.

The night before I had walked up to the campsite shop and bought a sort of flat bread and a tin which sported the picture of some form of sea creature. I was hoping for pilchards, but they turned out to be something related to the whelk family, chewy little salty squirts of the ocean, small parcels of snot that burst like an eye when you bit down on them. I ate my snot poppers later one by one, each bite a grimace of anticipation. Ahh, the fine dining options of the international explorer.

While I was buying the ingredients for my feast, I also used the payphone outside to call Mum again. My brother Dave was definitely in Yugoslavia. The last time he had called home he was north of where I was currently camped, somewhere between Dubrovnik and Split. Still, that constituted a piece of tarmac nearly two-hundred miles in length, and he could be located anywhere along that stretch. Assuming of course that he was still there. If I could find him, I planned to take a break from the road, have myself a little beachside vacation with him. Drink some beers and burn my shockingly pale back the same shade of scarlet as my chest.

Not far from the town of Budva I was forced inland again by the Bay of Kotor which moulded several long peninsulas out of the putty of the land to create long tendrils of bays, the resemblance of a Norwegian Fjord, transported two thousand miles and plonked unceremoniously down into the Balkans. Pretty little fishing docks and restaurants lined the road that ran only inches from the bay. Rounded sloping hills framed the scene.

I parked the bike outside a small, brightly painted restaurant and was directed to a table close to the water. My waiter was young, tall, and good-looking. He wasn't actively rude to me, but he was entirely disinterested in doing his job. He shambled around, eventually brought me a Coca-Cola and what might have been a ham sandwich and then disappeared. In the end I had to go inside to find him to pay.

It was a pattern of behaviour that would repeat itself during the remainder of my stay in Yugoslavia. I could only assume that the attitude was a hangover from the years of imposed communism. My waiter was going to get paid regardless of the service he provided, and so it was with the other shopkeepers and waiters, bank staff and folks who pumped petrol I encountered that year, they just went through the motions, delivered against the contract that employed them but took little interest or joy in anything they did.

I passed the port town of Dubrovnik on a hillside road that overlooked the pretty town. Rolling hills and tall pines surrounded the orange tiled roofs of the houses tightly cocooned between the foothills and the placid, boat speckled sea. The coast road and most of the towns there cling to the mile wide strip of land, trapped firmly between the spectacular sweep of the Adriatic on one side and the vertical sedimentary cliffs that tower like the unscalable sides of some gigantic battleship on the other. The roads along the coast were bumpy, dotted with old potholes and hasty repairs. It was like riding on a patchwork quilt of tarmac textures. It required an exhausting amount of constant concentration, to peer ahead in order to be able to ride around the bigger holes and avoid disaster.

I started to scan the road ahead for signs for campsites. As soon as I saw one, my pulse raced, and I pulled over immediately, parked the bike in the shade, and almost jogged into reception to see if they had checked in a scruffy looking English biker with the same surname as my own. The answer was a shake of the head.

Mile after weary mile I rode north up the coast. At every sign for a campsite, I would quickly park up, and jog up to reception expecting somebody to nod that, yes, somebody else called Wareing was indeed camped somewhere within their facility, marking the end of that day's ride and the reunion of two brothers.

But the further north I rode, and the more campsites I visited, the afternoon continued to wane, and my excitement slipped away and transitioned to disappointment. I finally had to admit to myself that I had long since given up the belief I would manage to find my brother.

I decided to just keep riding. There was no way I was going to find Dave. The whole idea had been ludicrous. How the hell had I thought I could just ride up the coast of Yugoslavia and bump into my brother. So stupid.

I would, instead, just keep riding on my own, towards Yugoslavia's northern border until the daylight dwindled and camp there, before beginning the long ride home alone, back to England. The sudden realization that I would have to ride all the way home alone made me suddenly homesick. I was still fatigued from my illness, and still a touch leaky in the trouser department. I was bored with my own company at last. As fast as I rode, a black cloud pursued me along the coast, a blot in the perfect blue of the sky.

I was preoccupied with these thoughts when I swept around a long curve, and there by the side of the dusty road, outside the gates of yet another camping site was parked a silver Moto Guzzi 850. It could only be Dave's.

I jumped on the brakes, indicated way too late, and cut across the road forcing a turd-coloured Lada to swerve and toot his pathetic horn. I pulled over onto the soft sand of the verge and parked the Suzuki next to the Guzzi. Just as I turned off the ignition and kicked the side stand down, Dave himself walked out of the gates accompanied by Novak Djokovic. Well, it wasn't actually Novak himself, but it looked just like him. Tall and athletic with a hairstyle last seen on a 1970's action man.

We had a hug. Me and Dave I mean, I hadn't yet been properly introduced to Novak. I assumed this was where

Dave was camping but he had been dropping Novak off for some reason. Dave was actually camped just outside the town of Makarska just a few miles down the road. How serendipitous. If he hadn't been running this errand on his bike, he wouldn't have been parked on the road, and I, having already abandoned any hope of finding him, would have ridden right past where he had actually been camped.

Dave set off on his Guzzi, and I followed him back to his site. I checked in at the shabby little reception and set up my now very tatty looking, home-repaired tent next to his. He introduced me to six or seven other Novak Djokovics, all camped in a cluster of tents around us.

They were all young, tall, tanned, good looking and athletic with legs like sculpted tree-trunks. They turned out to be part of a professional football team, here taking a few days with their girlfriends to make merry, drink, and make vertically challenged Englishmen look inadequate in shorts.

It was dinner time, so we took our leave of the Yugoslavian footballers for a while and walked into town. We found a restaurant that overlooked the insanely pretty Adriatic and sat at a table outside. The mountains behind us darkened first and then the sky faded to black around us. The warm wind wafted the hairs on our legs and shins in a delightful manner. Lights twinkled along the long curve of the promenade where handsome couples walked arm in arm.

We ordered ice cold beers and a Rostilj, a meat sharing platter so large and greasy I swear I felt the LDL, the bad cholesterol, swim straight from my stomach to instantly clog a major artery. We shared travel stories and laughed until our bellies ached, all the time eating our way through a steaming mound of Ćevapi, rich Serbian sausages, tender grilled chickens, pork neck tenderloin cutlets and juicy lamb chops, all seasoned in a sweet red pepper paprika barbeque sauce.

We drank beer upon beer and then staggered back to the campsite with greasy fingers, carrying our bloated stomachs on alcohol filleted and wobbly legs, stopping now and again to crease ourselves in laughter, recounting stories both old and new.

A Farewell

We stayed in Makarska for a few more days. We drank cold beers during the day and warm wine at night, always in the affable company of the footballing Yugoslavs and their girlfriends. I don't remember all of their names, far too much time has slipped by. Too many days, months and years have passed to irrevocably wipe the chalky details from the black board of my memory. But I do recall that there was a Mirsad, an Amela, there was John, who called himself 'great lover,' and Hari, who we called 'Hari Mata Hari.'

They had taken my brother under their protective wing when they had found out he was travelling alone, and they accepted me like an old friend for the short time I was with them. They helped us and guided us. We heard them talk about Tito, his name was everywhere, though in their case, it was without enthusiasm, usually with a mournful shake of their heads. This was a different generation, one born to look forwards, and to embrace, a modern future, not back towards the austerity and strange but familiar comfort of their parent's old regime.

These young Yugoslavs were sportsmen and women; better educated and wealthy in a way that their mothers and fathers had never had the opportunity to be. The old guard had gone forever, and they had no reason to not believe that fame and fortune lay, literally at their feet.

We knew the beers we drank every day were bought from the campsite shop; but the wine had a more mysterious provenance. Every evening one of the Yugoslavs would disappear with an empty, flimsy plastic two-litre flagon in hand into the darkened woods to the side of the campsite. Ten minutes would pass and then he or she would reappear with one bulging with something suspiciously resembling Rioja. We never found out where or how the transaction took place, but we were willing participants in the results.

We taught them some choice English words and they, in turn, taught us some Serbian. You know, the basics. The traveller's dictionary essentials:

Cheers— Živeli,

Thanks— Hvala,

Beer— Pivo,

Fuck off— Odjebi

We swam in the warm sea and bathed in the hot sunshine, we ate grilled sardines around the campfire and slept as late as our hangovers dictated. Jokes were told within the deep shadows cast by the full of the moon while the cicadas called in the hills. Language didn't seem to be a barrier, we all laughed together at each other's ridiculousness, joined together by a moment and a place rather than the need for complete understanding.

The days ran into one another, walks into town punctuated by the comfort of being surrounded by new friends. But of course, the clock of home never stopped ticking. Dave and I both had jobs to return to and time was always against us.

Finally, it was time to say our farewells, time to pack up and move on.

Without words we packed up our tents and belongings the next morning and carefully loaded the bikes. There were handshakes and back slaps and promises to stay in touch and then we were gone, the group of Djokovic lookalikes, madly waving, miniature specks in our mirrors.

We bounced over broken patches of road and swerved around holes and boulders all day in the searing heat as we journeyed north towards Austria. We passed Split and Zadar on the coast, the shining beacon of the Adriatic flashing constantly through the trees, tracking our speedy progress. But then we crossed the rattling Maslenicki Bridge and the tether that bound the sight of the sea to our path was severed. We were climbing into the hills and the first clouds were gathering.

All day long, as we skirted busy towns, and blasted through small mountain villages, I was either behind Dave's Guzzi listening to the regular thump, thump, of the big V-Twin or I was in front, navigating, checking my mirrors to make sure Dave and the yellow tinted headlight of the Guzzi were still following in my wake.

We were bound for the peaks of the Karawanks, part of the Southern Limestone Alps that sit with the weight of a leviathan across the border between Yugoslavia and Austria. There is a seven-kilometre-long tunnel through the Alps nowadays but back in the 1980's it was toward a lofty and twisty mountain pass you were forced to navigate. We had chosen the Loibl pass.

The temperature dropped as we ascended into the foothills, the jagged peaks distant and bathed in streaming cloud. At the next gas station, I pulled over and we emptied our pockets of Dinars in exchange for petrol. My hands were starting to chill in the cooler air of the mountain elevations, and I searched the bag strapped to the back of the bike for my gauntlets, first abandoned in the parking lot of the tractor tire outlet in Bulgaria. To my horror, they were nowhere to be found. I checked everywhere. I scoured between the travel documents and camera equipment in my tank bag, and even risked delving a hand into my panniers which, by this point of the journey had accrued sufficient DNA in the form of sweat stained t-shirts and shit stained underpants to have terraformed into a new species. I looked ever more frantically, but they were nowhere to be found. They must have come loose somewhere.

If I had been German or Dutch, I would have had two or three spare pairs, a glove for all seasons, but I was both poor and British, so I channelled my bulldog spirit and made do. I found some thick wool socks and with my little pocketknife I cut a hole for my thumbs to form oddly shaped mittens.

Mentally applauding my clever improvisation with toasty hands, we jumped back on the bikes. I had visions of appearing on Shark Tank or Dragon's Den, pitching my invention to the investors. Should I patent them as 'Sockens' or 'Mittocks?'

The Loibl pass has a chequered history. There has been a pass there since Roman times. It was deemed an important trade route between Vienna and the Port of Trieste and when Emperor Charles VI toured in the year 1728 he ordered the upper portions of the high pass to be improved. Two stone obelisks were erected at the peak to mark his visit and they stand there still, like two unseeing sentinels looking out for eternity at the valley below.

Under German occupation during WWII a 3,500-foot-long tunnel was built to avoid the tightest and most precarious turns closer to the summit, necessary to enable it to transport large and ponderous military vehicles. To build the tunnel, prisoners of war were forced into manual labour.

Under the command of Obersturmführer Julius Ludolf, inhumane conditions were imposed on the prisoners. Around forty prisoners died, and hundreds were rendered unable to work due to the constant beatings and torture. Rather than go through the trouble of transporting these poorly prisoners back down the mountain, many were executed on the spot by injecting those poor souls with petrol. It makes you ponder how such a noble and modern nation could take such a dark turn in its history.

It was a deeply sobering thought as we climbed through the hairpins and switchbacks of the peaks that towered into the sky all around us. The rain started to fall from a sky the colour of spilt oil. The peaks of the mountains were wreathed in a dense mist. Rainwater ran across the road, critically making deep pools on the apex of the tightest hairpins, causing the roads to be both slippery and treacherous.

The mountain roads of Yugoslavia left a lot to be desired. Gullies over ran with water and the cliffs at our elbows had eroded. The tarmac was rough and patchy. There were no streetlights and my visor fogged in the cold mountain air. I was forced to raise the visor to navigate the switchbacks and tight turns while avoiding the disaster of hitting one of the bigger and deeper ruts that lay across our path.

My eyes became sore from staring, wide-eyed ahead to look for loose boulders and a road surface that might surprise the unwary. The rain joined the mist to soak us through and I was forced to blink continuously to clear the streaming water from tired eyes, peering into the half-light of the mountain pass.

The leaden skies darkened as we approached the mouth of the tunnel and now my homemade mitten idea didn't seem quite so clever. The cold rainwater swiftly turned my repurposed woolly socks into damp and frosty sponges, and now my chapped hands were essentially plunged into small portable hand baths filled with ice.

The tunnel gave some temporary respite from the rain although on the Yugoslavian side the road conditions inside the tunnel were the worst that we had experienced. The roads were atrocious, broken concrete slabs and deep, suspension destroying potholes marked our path and we were forced to ride slow, to weave carefully around the worst of them.

We crossed the physical border with Austria halfway through the tunnel. It was clear where the actual border lay because on the Austrian side the road was instantly a smooth, painted stretch of tarmac that looked like it had been immaculately steam rolled just yesterday. We cleared passport control and customs a mile after we exited the tunnel. Dave and I exchanged an eye roll and a sigh of relief at being back inside the Europe we were accustomed to, and let the sodium vapor streetlights guide us safely back down the mountain.

We must have camped in Austria somewhere. I was cold and suffering once more. I wasn't sure if my bout of dysentery had returned but I was shivering and sick. Normally I can bring to mind every hotel, every campground but that night eludes my recall.

I do know that we must have set off again in the morning because I clearly recall the interminable misery of the next day. We rode the Autobahns of Germany north of

Munich. The clouds were so low and dense they touched the road, swept sheets of rainwater across the grey tarmac, it was like riding through a vast bowl of gruel. Rain swept in horizontal torrents and my sodden mittocks made me deeply sad.

It felt like we had already reached the end of the adventure. Every mile we were closer to home; my brothers red taillight and the throbbing exhaust note of the Moto Guzzi was a fishhook pulling me closer to the shore and the snare of home, work and the girlfriend I had left behind.

Like the spring steel of a grandfather clock, my time in Europe was uncoiling, counting down the seconds, measured in the rhythmic drum of rain on my helmet and the racing droplets of rain across my breath fogged visor.

I struggled to concentrate. My head ached; my guts swam. I was itchy and feverish, terribly cold, and uncomfortable. I could no longer feel my hands. It seemed that yesterday's dream of becoming stupidly rich on Dragon's Den for an innovative approach to mitten design was rapidly slipping through my numb and chilblained fingers.

Past Munich and Stuttgart we rode through the half-lit deluge of the day. If we hadn't lingered so long in Yugoslavia, drinking wine with the footballers in the sunshine, we could have stopped and found a comfortable hotel in which to dry off and drink beer while we waited for the weather to change. But we had passed on that privilege. All we had left was a dash to the coast.

I was daydreaming again and was worried that I might slip into sleep. It was a challenge to keep up a good speed on the bikes, they shimmied in the standing water and slowed as we were forced to plough through deep puddles that formed on the edges of the Autobahn. The trucks blasted past us ensuring we were soaked from above, below and from all sides.

Finally, just as I thought I might have to flash Dave and get him to pull of the Autobahn, through the grey of the day, I saw Dave's indicator come on. He must have been suffering as much as myself and had clearly had enough and chosen to call it a day and just get off the Autobahn.

The indicator startled me and I had to snatch at the front brake to keep from riding into the back of the Guzzi. I think that I had been close to sleep again, lulled to slumber by the numbing cold and the repetition of a landscape turned opaque and dismal by the driving rain, towns and cities, hills and farms pushed into the background of deluge.

I followed Dave's Guzzi into a small town. Who knew where we were? Somewhere close to the Rhine for sure and reasonably north, we had ridden all day although the sky had resembled dusk the entire time. Duisberg? Bergisch Gladbach? Mülheim-Kärlich? Who knew, there are a thousand such towns in northern Germany. The town looked dirty in the reflected puddles, too tired and too narrow.

Dave spotted a small guest house with glowing windows and pulled immediately into the drive. I followed, like a drowned rat, or a nodding child drawn to the piper.

At the end of a path, to the right of the welcomingly lit windows of the restaurant, lay three low squat garages. Two already had cars parked, but the one to the left lay dry and empty. With the rain still pelting down we parked the bikes in the empty one, I threw my mittocks into a garbage can by the door and we dragged our sodden luggage into the hotel reception.

"Ein Doppelzimmer bitte?"

The middle aged and portly bearded man at the reception gave us a quizzical look. Two extremely sodden British bikers, clad in leather, arriving together in his small rural village and asking for a room with only one double bed, we were probably not representative of his target clientele. He couldn't make up his mind who to hand the key to, you could see the open panic in his eyes, so I reached across and snatched it from his cringing palm.

We dumped our stuff in the room that held our double bed. The room was small but warm, the bed covered in a puffy duvet and an old-fashioned hand embroidered counterpane. I was tempted to immediately clamber in amongst the pillows and covers and shiver myself to sleep but, tired and cold as I was, I was also ravenous.

The bar was busy, and word had obviously spread of the unusual guests staying in room fünf. All heads turned as we entered and there were nudges and the sound of muted hilarity. We found an empty table and sat down facing each other like the lovers everybody had assumed we must be. We ordered pepper steaks and two enormous steins of frothing beer. The steaks were gargantuan, juicy and fiery with the heat of the pepper sauce. The calories restored me somewhat to myself.

With the steak finished I realized I was still hungry. I looked at the menu but didn't need another full meal, just a snack. In my best German I risked a venture off the colloquial piste and attempted to ask for a fried egg on toast.

"Ei mit brot bitte."

Unfortunately, I didn't know the German word for either fried or toast, so, ten minutes later, what was placed on the table, accompanied by a puzzled looked from both my server and the locals around us was a raw egg cracked onto a piece of cold bread.

With cold egg yolk dripping down my chin, me and Dave walked up the stairs and climbed into bed together. I was asleep instantly. Warm and toasty, snuggled under the heavy duvet. I was back, dreaming of the touch of the warm sun on an Adriatic beach.

A banging on the bedroom door woke us both with a start. Dave opened the door with a wide yawn in his grubby underpants to find the chubby receptionist standing awkwardly in the doorway. The man looked sheepish and embarrassed to have woken these two young, bed-sharing men. And now, here was one of them blinking in the light from the hallway, standing, almost naked, scratching himself with sleep and confusion on his face.

"Whaddaya want," Dave mumbled.

"Would you gentlemen please move your motorcycles?" he stammered in an accent redolent of a German Terminator.

One of his long-term guests had returned, in the middle of the night, to discover two bikes taking up the garage space reserved for his precious Audi. Rather than let the two 'gentlemen' sleep and ask them to move their bikes in the morning, the asshole had the temerity to wake us both up at 3am and ask us to go back into the rain. It was then that we looked at the clock on the bedside to realize it was only 7:45 in the evening.

We hopped into damp trousers and shrugged ourselves into soggy jackets and found ourselves back in the cold rain pushing heavy motorcycles out of a bone-dry garage, muttering, and cursing all things Teutonic.

An Ending

In the morning, my fever had passed. I think that was all I needed. A good steak, a cold beer, a decent warm bed, and a raw egg. Our leathers had dried to a crisp on the radiators, they would need a gallon of Neat's-foot leather conditioner when we got home, but the inside lining of my helmet was still disturbingly damp and would remain so for the remainder of the trip.

We walked down to enjoy some strong black coffee, sharp orange juice and a huge buffet breakfast. There were hearty brots and brötchen decorated with butter, sweet jams and local honey; thinly sliced salamis, sausages and hams; allgau-emmental, limburger, and cambozola cheeses, smoky and pungent. Somebody in the kitchen had even figured out how to cook an egg. We ate like kings and then, to get payback for the previous night's disturbance, we over filled our helmets with what would later become lunch.

The rain had stopped, the day was warm and dry. The town looked pretty in the morning sunshine. The streets were drying and the buildings, brick gothic and ancient, sat squat under steaming pitched roofs.

We hit the Autobahn and made fast progress north. We passed a corn field and saw three roe deer standing like spectres, seemingly afloat as they waded through the low mist that clung to the furrows of the field. They watched us, standing stock still, only their twitching ears betraying their existence and vitality.

We crossed the border back into Holland and stopped at a rest place by the side of the road. We sat at a table and ate our pilfered lunch and then it was time to separate again. Dave had to catch a ferry back to the UK, and I was to ride on, to visit a Dutch friend in Eindhoven.

A day later I crossed the channel once more. This time from Calais, landing in Dover in the early hours of a Friday morning. The port was already busy, teeming with cars heading out to the continent. I rode down from the ferry ramp muttering, "ride on the left, on the left, on the left," as I navigated the bollards and small roundabouts that lead new arrivals away from the docks.

I picked up the M20 outside Folkestone and wound the throttle back. Now that I was back in England, I just wanted the journey to end. I still had a hole in my jeans where the knife had slipped through. My tent was busted, my exhaust cracked, and the oil still dripped from the cylinder head gasket of my trusty Suzuki GS1000G.

My panniers were stuffed full of filthy clothes. At times I could feel them moving around back there. The inside of my sleeping bag smelt worse than a bucket of prawns that had been left out in the sun. The fairing and headlight of the bike had killed so many bugs they looked like they were covered in thick black coating of fur.

I was exhausted but content. I had the road dust, pollen, and grime of nearly four-thousand miles in the pores of my skin and what little remained of my hair. The parts of me that had not been covered in leather and denim had been scorched walnut brown by the touch of an unfamiliar sun.

My eyes had borne witness to the sights, smells and sounds of eight different countries and two continents.

Across Holland, Germany, Austria, Yugoslavia, Hungary, Bulgaria, Turkey and Greece, the big Suzuki had pulled me tirelessly across borders, up mountains and across rivers, whose names I had only previously dreamed of seeing. Together we had crossed all of the Balkan states that were, back then, part of Yugoslavia: Slovenia, Bosnia and Herzegovina, Croatia, Montenegro, Kosovo, North Macedonia and Serbia.

The Suzuki and I had ridden across the Bosporus and dipped our collective toes and tires into the mystery that was Asia. Through rural villages lost to time and through vast cities that sought to snare us the Suzuki had safely carried me.

It had been eye opening as travel often can, and should, be. Confusing, frightening, enlightening and wildly amusing in almost equal measures, all done on a shoestring budget of cash and time and in a place and in an era that has long since vanished. One of paper maps and no smart phones, no Siri or Google. When large swathes of Europe were hidden and off-limits behind the Iron Curtain of Soviet era communism. When *all* land borders were closed, and currencies changed as swiftly as the cultures and languages you encountered.

In only a couple of days I would be back at work, climbing poles for British Telecom and thinking of where to punish myself the following year.

As stated, this story took place in 1986. I have already alluded to the tense friction that I found to be evident in Yugoslavia shortly after Tito's death.

Only five years after I returned from this adventure, in 1991, all of the resentments and religious bigotries inevitably boiled over into conflict. The war in Yugoslavia was not a single conflict, rather a series of ethnic battles, wars of independence, and insurgencies. Both political and religious in nature, the war would rage for ten years and end in the loss of 130,000 Yugoslavian lives and the displacement of millions.

The Yugoslav Wars were also marked by heinous war crimes, genocide, crimes against humanity, ethnic cleansing, and mass wartime rape. These words became staples of every news bulletin as the country slowly shattered itself into six independent countries on our nightly TV screens. Names we should never have known became suddenly notorious. Goran Hadzic, Slobodan Milosevic, and Ratko Mladic all stood trial at The Hague after the war, charged by the UN war crimes tribunal.

Goran Hadzic escaped sentencing by being lucky, or unlucky enough, depending upon your viewpoint to succumbing to brain cancer. Slobodan Milosevic died of a sudden and unexpected heart attack in his cell before his sentence could be announced and Ratko Mladic, the

'Butcher of Bosnia,' was given a life sentence and still, to this day, resides in a cell in The Hague.

A last footnote, if you will. After we returned to the UK my brother Dave kept in sporadic touch with our Yugoslavian friends, but from the moment the war began, we never again heard from them. Mirsad, Amela, John 'great lover.' Hari 'Mata Hari,' they were, of course, all of prime fighting age. It seemed unlikely they had been spared from the violence.

A stark reminder that a country is so much more than simply names and borders, its politics, its religions, its culture and history, architecture, and language. All of those elements matter of course, but surely what really makes a country what it is, what defines its personality and the manner in which it interacts with its neighbours and the greater world beyond its borders, is its people.

My cucumber munching gardeners for example, my onyx-eyed, 'very good, very cheap' guide, my Turkish shopkeeper, Andre the Giant's bigger brother who terrified me and saved me in equal measure, and of course, our Yugoslavian footballing friends from around the campfire.

Friends who drank flagons of wine of doubtful provenance together, hugged and cried and laughed, like tomorrow would never come.

THE END

So, you made it through the Iron Curtain...

Ready to head north? I mean way north—through snow, silence, and some frankly questionable decisions involving reindeer, Norwegian tunnels, and your humble narrator's ever-deteriorating common sense.

Get Book Two: *A Fast Bike to North Cape*

https://geni.us/BM_NorthCape

Prefer a signed copy with a free bookmark and a custom sticker? Order direct from the author

A FAST BIKE TO NORTH CAPE

https://geni.us/BM_NorthCape

And don't forget to check out my other books available on both Amazon and my website.

The Petrolhead Travelogues

https://www.andycwareing.com/

ANDY C WAREING

Andy is a multi-genre Indie author, originally from the United Kingdom. He has lived with his wife Paula and their two dogs Archie and Pi in Atlanta GA for the last fifteen years (with the exception of a year in Spain/UK during the pandemic). At heart always British, he loved living in the U.S.A. but will never vocalize the American pronunciations of basil, banana, or tomato. He currently lives in leafy Somerset, a land of apples, cider, and weather so perpetually wet, 'wellies' are considered formal wear.

Please take a moment to visit my website to see more books and get great discounts and offers.

ANDY C WAREING

Be a stalker and follow me on Facebook, Goodreads, or my author page on Amazon for updates on new projects:

facebook.com/andycwareing

goodreads.com/author/show/21017809.Andy_C_Warei
ng

amazon.com/author/andycwareing

email: author@andycwareing.com

Made in the USA
Monee, IL
10 March 2026

45867726R00109